CHRIS & NANCY

CHRIS & NANCY

THE TRUE STORY OF THE BENOIT MURDER-SUICIDE & PRO WRESTLING'S COCKTAIL OF DEATH

IRVIN MUCHNICK

ECW Press

Published by ECW Press, 2120 Queen Street East, Suite 200,
Toronto, Ontario, Canada M4E 1E2
416.694.3348 / info@ecwpress.com

LIBRARY AND ARCHIVES CANADA CATALOGUING IN PUBLICATION

Muchnick, Irvin
Chris & Nancy : the true story of the Benoit murder-suicide and pro wrestling's
cocktail of death / Irvin Muchnick.

ISBN 978-1-55022-902-8

1. Benoit, Chris, 1967–2007. 2. Benoit, Nancy. 3. Wrestlers — Canada — Biography.
4. Murder — Georgia — Fayetteville. 5. Suicide — Georgia — Fayetteville. 6. Wrestling.
I. Title. II. Title: Chris and Nancy.

GV1196.B45M83 2009   796.812092   C2009-902533-7

Cover design: David Gee
Cover images: Mike Lano; Mike Mastrandrea; ECW Press archives
Text design and photo section: Tania Craan
Typesetting: Mary Bowness
Printing: Victor Graphics   1   2   3   4   5

ECW PRESS
ecwpress.com

Grow up your forty [years old] for mighty sakes
get off the stuff it's obvious im probably not the only one
who can see and we both know the [World Wrestling
Entertainment] wellness program is a joke.
Nancy Benoit to Chris Benoit
text message, May 10, 2007

The scandal isn't what's illegal. It's what's legal.
Michael Kinsley

Contents

Foreword by Phil Mushnick

I SHARE AN UNINTENDED BADGE of honor with Irvin Muchnick: if Vince McMahon and World Wrestling Entertainment ever put on paper something similar to President Nixon's "enemies list," both Irv and I would be on it, top ten.

Pro wrestling, by industry design, and hard journalism are oil and water. Irv, like me, only far more often, focuses on this industry's death trap, not its magic show. That's one reason why I hope *Chris & Nancy* gets widely read — and, more important, acted upon.

Before I go any further, a clarification, one both of us have made dozens of times over the past dozen years: beyond our professions, Irv Muchnick and Phil Mushnick are not related. Irv's paternal grandparents and his then six-year-old future uncle, Sam Muchnick (who would become the legendary St. Louis promoter and long-time president of the National Wrestling Alliance), docked at Baltimore, where their surname was transliterated to "Muchnick," with a "c." I'm a third-generation Staten Islander (my ancestors came over on the ferry), and no one's quite sure (or much cares) why or when Mushnick became Mushnick.

Irv was living in New York in the early 1980s when I became the media sports columnist for the *New York Post*. At the time there were sports anchors on local TV newscasts — Warner Wolf on WCBS, Spencer Christian on WABC — who frequently aired WWF clips as legitimate sports highlights. Irv was the first of my readers to warn me that my mere outrage could not contain this phenomenon.

And indeed, by 1985 Andy Warhol and the downtown Manhattan demimonde were seizing the proverbial fifteen minutes to proclaim wrestling the newest manifestation of "camp" art. In March of that year, when McMahon produced the first *WrestleMania* on pay-per-view, two of his key shills were Dick Ebersol (the future president of NBC Sports and co-impresario of the disastrous XFL football league) and Bob Costas (having taken a break from his otherwise well-earned position as the "conscience of sportscasting").

Three years later Irv Muchnick published a devastating profile of the sick Von Erich wrestling family of Texas (one son died accidentally from prescription drugs, one was a drug suicide, two shot themselves to death). The piece would be selected for the anthology *Best Magazine Articles: 1988*; not best wrestling magazine articles or best sports magazine articles, but the best magazine articles of any kind. "Born-Again Bashing With the Von Erichs" was the first serious attempt at legitimate long-form narrative journalism on what quickly became a pandemic of occupation-related deaths in American junk entertainment.

A few years after that, now living in California, Irv

stayed at my house while he tracked down the cover-up of how Jimmy "Superfly" Snuka probably killed his girlfriend in a Pennsylvania motel room in 1983. The Von Erich and Snuka stories would be included in Irv's 2007 collection, *Wrestling Babylon*.

In the 1990s, as night follows day, scandal wracked WWF. The original "mark" doctor, George Zahorian, got busted by the feds for distributing steroids like Tic Tacs. McMahon himself was indicted (but acquitted at trial). His company, competing in a race to the bottom with Ted Turner's deeper-pocketed World Championship Wrestling, clawed back with R-rated programming, which glommed the crotch-grabbing wit of "Degeneration X" onto the perverse family pitch of the Hulkamania era.

In the course of our long friendship, Muchnick and I haven't always seen eye to eye. He can't always be right, ya know. But I've leaned on him for information, insight, and inspiration far more often than he has on me. I simply appreciate and admire Irv's work for projecting a vision of wrestling's dark side in a way that transcends the subject. His larger canvas isn't wrestling. It's how all of late-empire America has been *wrestlingized*.

In my *Post* column, Vince McMahon's sleaze mill gets less attention than it once did. This fact does not reflect that there are bigger fish to fry so much as it acknowledges this sad triumph of wrestling values throughout sports and culture. In years to come, for example, we're certain to see more and more veterans of baseball's steroid era dying young, like Ken Caminiti and like the hundreds of wrestlers both before and after him. The ESPN TV, radio, and magazine brands — not to mention sports talk in general, and even national political discourse — all subscribe to the puerile "attitude" playbook pioneered by WWE. As a critic, I no longer need to note that fringe programming foretells the content of the mainstream. The future is now, and crude is in, and not likely to fade.

Meanwhile, from his own perspective, Muchnick is still throwing facts into the fire, still connecting the dots between the sacred cows of respectable society and the WrestleWorld they collude with. I'm glad he is. The Benoit murder-suicide was one of the most sensational crime stories of 2007, and it cried out for the scrutiny of someone with a longer attention span and more intellectual integrity than the local authorities, the media, and Congress brought to bear on it. If you can read what Irv has dug up and continue to turn your head, then your powers of denial exceed mine.

Introduction

THE HORROR OF CHRIS BENOIT's June 2007 murder-suicide rampage is as good a reminder as any that it is high time to demystify professional wrestling. For too long, this industry has been inoculated from scandal by a banal mystique, the widespread belief that it is an enterprise whose offbeat rhythms simply cannot be mastered, and one whose players' motives lie beyond ordinary human understanding. Baloney and double baloney. Beneath the carny lingo and Mafioso code of silence rests a conventional profit-driven sector of show business, studded not only with glory-seeking performers but also with television executives, writers, technicians, chic-seeking kitsch kings, two-faced politicians. This is nothing less than the Periodic Table of the Elements of mainstream American pop culture. "Sports entertainment" is sports and entertainment, only more so.

The industry's dominant company, World Wrestling Entertainment — controlling more than ninety-five per-cent of the North American market and a vast majority worldwide — has grown into a multinational with more than a billion dollars in capitalization. It features an accompanying dark side as broad as a half-moon, hidden in plain sight. The brainchild of Vincent Kennedy McMahon, trailer-park incorrigible turned Forbes 400 squatter, WWE flowered in Connecticut, the same greenhouse that produced Phineas Taylor Barnum. The state's former governor, Lowell Weicker (once upon a time a hero of the Senate Watergate Committee), is a charter member of the WWE board of directors. In the 1990s, when McMahon was sinking under the first round of steroid and other scandals in what was then called the World Wrestling Federation, Weicker had helped rehabilitate his image with an appointment to a prominent position with the Connecticut branch of the Special Olympics.

In May 2007, a month before Benoit strangled his wife, Nancy, snapped their seven-year-old son Daniel's neck, and hanged himself, Vince McMahon delivered the commencement address at Sacred Heart University in Fairfield, Connecticut. SHU is the New England region's second-largest Catholic university. Vince McMahon's wife, Linda, the chief executive officer of WWE, is on the SHU board of trustees. As the university explained it, "Using self-deprecating humor to explain his choice as recipient of a Doctor of Humane Letters Degree and commencement speaker, McMahon . . . left most graduates and those in the audience with a sense of hope that anything is possible, even in the face of overwhelming obstacles." The mother of the student government president, in a sound bite no doubt crafted by the campus public relations department, called McMahon "a good choice for the school considering how he started his career and how he has parlayed it into this multimillion-dollar organization."

In sum, ladies and gentlemen, girls and boys, you *can* tell the players without a scorecard.

And enough with the Talmudic musings about how to categorize wrestling; they are irrelevant to whether the benefits of unregulated junk spectacle trump the public-health cesspool that "sports entertainment" has turned into. In 1982 a Hollywood star, Vic Morrow, and two Vietnamese-American child actors were killed in a gruesome late-night helicopter mishap during the filming of an action sequence of *The Twilight Zone: The Movie*. Reforms of filmmaking standards and California child-labor laws quickly followed. By contrast, Nancy and Chris Benoit were approximately the ninth and tenth of the approximately twenty-one wrestlers and in-ring personalities who died before their fiftieth birthdays in the year 2007 alone. Some scores or hundreds of others fill parallel lists over the past several decades — choose your time frame and methodology. Dave Meltzer, publisher of the authoritative *Wrestling Observer Newsletter*, said the list of eighty-nine deaths under the age of fifty, from 1985 to 2006, in my earlier book, *Wrestling Babylon*, was "incomplete, to be sure." Giving the numbers the best context I have seen, Meltzer drew up a list of sixty-two young deaths in "major league" wrestling organizations from 1996 to 2007.

The profile and tabloid details of the Benoit case shed a useful light on a generation-long legacy of shame; to dismiss this — and the probability that wrestling's drug-and-lifestyle deviances, induced from the very top, are major factors in the equation — is to make scoundrels' arguments.

Yet here is what has changed as a result of Benoit: almost nothing. Dissecting how that came to be is the

CHRIS & NANCY

second mission of this book. The first mission is to compile a comprehensive and accurate history of what happened in Fayette County, Georgia.

Toward that end, I strove to distinguish this book from others about wrestling by sticking to the public record as much as possible, and by emphasizing that if that turns out to be a problem, it is a problem shared by fans and non-fans alike. For example, everyone has an opinion on the significance, or lack thereof, of the 59-to-1 ratio of testosterone to epitestosterone in Benoit's postmortem toxicology tests. The few people who want to believe that such a finding tells us very little are far outnumbered by the many people who know that it tells us a lot; it's just that the few add more heat to the discussion than the many add light. While in other areas of life we may need fewer facts, wider-ranging intuition, and a spirit of live-and-let-live, wrestling has reached the point where it needs more facts — facts tethered to accountability — and less paralysis by analysis.

No, the butler didn't do it; Christopher Michael Benoit did. But honest scrutiny of what transpired before and after can demonstrate how WWE, as desperate and cagey as any gun or tobacco lobbyist, pulled the strings to ensure that wrestling's death pandemic would remain unaddressed. In real estate, the key is "location, location, location." In the Benoit story, the most fertile ground is "timeline, timeline, timeline." WWE's published timeline was as phony as its match results, and simultaneously far less entertaining and more illuminating.

To the question, "Was there a Benoit conspiracy?", we have a clear answer: you bet there was. It was a conspiracy between those who care too much about wrestling and those who care too little. The first group consists of

16

the fans who enjoy the pageantry and the people who profit from them. The second group consists of those who can't be bothered, except possibly to blow hard on cue whenever a comment, no matter how ill-informed, is deemed fashionable.

Like everyone else, I'll take my best stab at what it all means, but even this is only the second draft of history. The most important step is simply to cut through all the taboos that make wrestling an appropriate subject to cluck about, but not to study for its off-the-charts human fallout and for its seedy but pseudo-respectable big-business DNA. I submit that anything to which millions of people devote blocks of time every week is serious. Clusters of deaths are serious.

Let's tell and retell the Chris Benoit story in the hope that it will eventually make enough of the right people care in just the right amounts.

CHAPTER 1

"They've Killed the Family!"

THE FIRST PERSON TO ENCOUNTER the dead bodies of Chris Benoit's wife and their seven-year-old son, at around 2:45 p.m. Monday, June 25, 2007, was the next-door neighbor. Holly Schrepfer ran out of the house screaming to two Fayette County Sheriff's officers on the driveway outside, "Daniel and Nancy have been murdered! They've killed the family!"

At 1:35, Deputy Donna Mundy and Lieutenant Larry Alden had pulled up to the front of the Benoits' property in unincorporated Fayetteville, Georgia, in response to a call nineteen minutes earlier to the county 911 Communications Center. The cops faced an electronically locked double-iron gate separating a stacked stone wall from the circular driveway, which was set off nearly 200 feet from the main road. (The whole plot measured more than eight acres, typical for this area.) Mundy tried the call box outside the gate: no answer.

The officers noted that the fence on either side of the gate could be easily scaled. But the more significant obstacle to access was the presence of two German shepherd guard dogs roaming the front lawn near the gate and menacing anyone who might dare to traverse it.

Deputy Mundy had 911 dispatcher Chris Nations ask a World Wrestling Entertainment security consultant, Dennis Fagan, if anyone knew the gate pass code and how to pacify the dogs. Fagan had made the original emergency call. After checking with other WWE people, he reported back that while he couldn't come up with a pass code, he did learn that the neighbor to the left of the Benoits' house took care of the dogs whenever the family was away. This set of exchanges, including intervals between follow-up calls, lasted the better part of an hour.

The officers found Holly Schrepfer at home. Before joining them on the return to the Benoits' gate, Holly called Nancy. As had been the case for days, there was no answer.

Shortly after 2:30, Holly was climbing over the fence and calming the dogs. Their names were Carny and Highspot, inside jokes from Chris and Nancy's careers in professional wrestling. A carny, or carnival figure, refers to the sport's roots in the nineteenth-century big top, and its reliance ever since on a jargon ("mark" to signify a naive fan, "work" as a synonym for staging something fake, "kayfabe" for the overall con) comprehensible only to insiders. A "highspot" is an aerial maneuver in a wrestling match. During the two decades in which Chris Benoit rose to become one of wrestling's biggest stars, his signature highspot was a spectacular diving head butt from the top rope, sometimes called the Swan Dive.

Holly ushered the German shepherds through the unlocked door on the side of the garage leading into the house. The door led up a short flight of stairs to a mudroom where the dogs were kept in portable kennels. Holly locked up Carny and Highspot.

It was a warm early-summer afternoon in North

Georgia, temperature in the low 80s Fahrenheit. The central air conditioning system in the Benoit house was off, which made the odor hanging in the air, powerful but indistinct, more stagnant and intense.

With foreboding, Holly called out, "Nancy? Daniel?"

Holly ascended two flights to the upper level to look in Daniel's bedroom. The decor was dominated by posters and action figures of his wrestling father; on the dresser lay two toy replica championship belts. Holly found little Daniel, in a long-sleeve blue SpongeBob T-shirt, and pajama pants with a soccer-and-baseball design, lying in bed on his stomach, his left cheek on the pillow over turned-down covers. Next to him were two stuffed Winnie-the-Poohs and a book, *My First Bible* — a children's edition of the New Testament — propped atop his extended right hand. His right leg was bent, with the foot touching the left knee. As Holly got closer, she could see that Daniel wasn't just sleeping. His face was discolored. Dried-up foam was crusted around his mouth and nose.

Holly gasped and scrambled down one flight of stairs. She knew that Nancy kept a home office and liked to watch television in a room above the garage. That room, too, was strewn with wrestling memorabilia: framed photos, plaques, baseball caps promoting *WrestleManias* past.

There Holly found Nancy lying on her right side on the hardwood floor, a red fringed throw rug covering everything except her head and feet. She faced the wall between the sitting area and a wet bar. A pillow, askew, leaned against a messy head of brunette hair. Another Bible, a regular adult edition with a burgundy cover, lay alongside her. Nancy was in a white tank top and blue striped pajama bottoms. Her hands were tied together behind her back, at shoulder-blade level, with coaxial cable. A second cable, along with a small white rope, extended from there and wrapped around her neck. Her feet were bound with the cord from an electric charger, secured by black tape. Nancy's face was blue and black, her stomach bloated; her arms were already in an advanced state of decomposition.

Holly hurried down the steps, through the mudroom, and out the garage side door, yelling to Deputy Mundy and Lieutenant Alden that Daniel and Nancy had been murdered.

The officers told Holly to stay put in the driveway while they went inside and followed her directions to the two bodies. After confirming her discoveries, they searched the entire house, eventually making their way to the basement, which doubled as a home gym.

At 2:48 — traumatized, isolated, and worried about the officers' safety — Holly punched 911 on her cell phone.

"They asked me to hop the fence because they have attack dogs and I went in and someone had — the little boy and the mom are dead," Holly explained breathlessly to the dispatcher. "And so I ran out to scream to them but then they went in the house but they haven't come out yet. Are they OK?" She added, "I didn't see Mr. Benoit. I don't know where he is. I didn't want to go down in the basement for some reason. He might be dead."

The 911 dispatcher called the sheriff's dispatcher, who made contact with the cops inside the house. They assured Holly they were OK.

They were in the basement, where Chris was, indeed, also dead. They found him sitting upright on a bench facing a Magnum Fitness weight machine. He was shirtless, wearing red gym shorts and socks and sneakers. His left leg was extended, his right leg bent at the knee, foot tucked under his left thigh. The black nylon weight machine cable was around his neck; a strip of a white towel was underneath to keep the cable from cutting the skin.

Chris was being held in sitting position by the cable, which passed through pulleys attached to 150 pounds of weight. The weight stack on the machine had been supplemented by two forty-pound dumbbells on top. The weight was lifted and kept from going slack by Benoit's own 220 pounds of body weight, plus two additional ten-pound dumbbells, which appeared to have dropped from his grip to the floor. Clearly, he had put much thought and masochistic discipline into hanging himself in near-perfect equipoise, not only to ensure a successful hanging but also to maximize the pain he must have intended to inflict on himself in the process. When the dumbbells had dropped, his body rotated right, just over the spot on the floor where two cell phones, his and Nancy's, rested next to a water bottle filled with green tea. Also on the floor was an empty bottle of Dynamite Vineyards 2004 merlot.*

Inspection of all the doors and windows revealed no sign of forced entry.

* * *

---

* The death certificates would list the causes of death as "strangulation" for Nancy, "suffocation" for Daniel, and "hanging" for Chris. With respect to Daniel, though media reports routinely cited "suffocation," "asphyxiation," and similar terms, the autopsy report of the Georgia Bureau of Investigation Crime Lab would say "cervical compression." That seems to me somewhat different — and more consistent with the damage that would be inflicted by Chris's applying on Daniel a version of the "Crippler Crossface" wrestling hold, as investigators speculated he did. (This as opposed to, say, choking Daniel or holding a pillow over his face.) The GBI medical examiner, Dr. Kris Sperry, said in an email that "any differences between the GBI reports and the death certificates (which were issued by the Fayette County Coroner) are solely the responsibility of the Coroner, and not the GBI." A copy of the GBI autopsy report is included in the companion disk. See "Order the DVD" at the back of this book.

WWE security man Fagan's first contact with 911 had come nearly two hours after his company, Andrews International, made the apparent final WWE-generated call to the Benoit home, at 11 a.m. A little more than an hour later, Fagan called someone in the sheriff's office who advised him that the way to proceed was to ask 911 for a "welfare check." The summons to law enforcement marked the beginning of the end of a drama that stretched across more than sixty hours.

Two days earlier, Saturday the 23rd, Chris Benoit had missed his appearance at a wrestling show in Beaumont, Texas, following a day and an evening of conflicting messages in conversations with concerned fellow wrestlers and the WWE front office. These conversations were surely after the murder of Nancy (which most likely took place on Friday night). At least some, and probably all, of them also succeeded the murder of Daniel (which most likely took place early Saturday). Chris's basic cover story that day was that he was pinned down at home in Georgia, where he said Nancy and Daniel had food poisoning and were vomiting blood. Chris promised his colleagues and bosses that he would get his wife and son cared for and join the WWE Texas tour with dispatch.

But Benoit did not turn up in Houston either late that night or the next day, Sunday the 24th. On Sunday night WWE staged one of its biggest shows of the year, *Vengeance — Night of Champions*, broadcast globally on cable and satellite systems to pay-per-view subscribers. The original script for *Vengeance* called for Chris to win his match and, with it, the championship of ECW, one of the company's three "brands" of wrestling troupes. With Chris's no-show, the match lineup had to be scrambled. The live crowd of 15,000-plus at the Toyota Center and the pay-per-view audience were told that Benoit had been detained by a family emergency.

Some wrestlers had bad histories of missing bookings, often because of alcohol or substance abuse. But the fanatically reliable Benoit was not one of them. Seven years earlier he'd even wrestled for months with a broken neck before finally succumbing to cervical fusion surgery, which sidelined him for most of a year. He never missed a show.

In the early morning hours of Sunday, more than sixteen hours before the first bell of *Vengeance*, Chris had sent a series of text messages from his and Nancy's cell phones to the cells of two colleagues, wrestler Chavo Guerrero and referee (and ex-wrestler) Scott Armstrong. The messages contained two repeated and cryptic snippets of information: "My physical address is 130 Green Meadow Lane, Fayetteville, Georgia, 30215" and "The dogs are in the enclosed pool area. Garage side door is open." Benoit was saying farewell and giving directions to the scene of the carnage, but that meaning would become crystal-clear only with 20/20 hindsight.*

Dennis Fagan revealed little of this background in his Monday afternoon call to the authorities. One possible explanation for this is that wwe executives had not thoroughly briefed Fagan. Yet when the 911 dispatcher Cathy Crenshaw asked, "What is your emergency?", among Fagan's first words were, "I run the security for World Wrestling."

Fagan said Chris had missed the show last night, which was unlike him, as he was "very religious" about his work commitments.

---

* The sheriff's report referred to Scott Armstrong as "Scott James."

A retired New York City Police Department detective, Fagan held the title "Executive Director, East Coast Anti-Piracy and Special Events" for Andrews International, which described itself as "a full service provider of security and risk mitigation services, and one of the ten largest private security service providers in the United States." Later, according to Detective Ethon Harper, who authored the report closing the Fayette County investigation of the Benoit case, the sheriff's office would ask Fagan and Andrews International no detailed questions about how the company came to be involved in the hectic events of a weekend during which a star performer for an Andrews client missed two straight appearances, including a championship match on a pay-per-view show. "I spoke with someone at Andrews International to see what type of business they were," Harper told me. "I also wanted to confirm that the number on the phone records was one of their phone numbers. It was."

In an email to me, WWE's vice president of corporate communications, Gary Davis, fell well short of confirming that Fagan "ran" WWE security operations. "Dennis Fagan is employed by a security firm utilized by WWE. He assisted us in trying to contact Chris Benoit on the weekend in question," Davis said. Davis did not clarify whether the single record of Andrews International's involvement, the 11 a.m. Monday call to the Benoit home, qualified as a "weekend" effort, but the statement at least suggests that Fagan had a somewhat more substantial role, in turn raising suspicion on why he would give inaccurate information in his series of calls to 911 and why the sheriff would not have asked him an additional substantive question or two.

Whatever Fagan's level of authority or involvement,

his 911 calls exhibited a lack of intimate knowledge of the events leading up to them. "At three o'clock this morning there was a message left for one of the other wrestlers," Fagan said to the dispatcher. "And basically it says, 'The dogs are in the backyard. The back door is open. Goodbye.' And that's it." In fact, there were multiple messages from Benoit, not "a message"; and they were not "this morning" but the previous morning — well over thirty hours before the first call to 911.

Fagan's citation of the wrong day for the text messages was not an isolated slip of the tongue. Later in the same, initial 911 call, Fagan reiterated, "That message was at three o'clock this morning."

Either WWE misinformed Fagan of the timing of the final text messages or he was confused — or lying.

The sheriff's report closing the investigation would erroneously state that Fagan told 911 that Benoit "left a text message for a wrestling co-worker around 3 a.m. on Sunday, June 24, 2007." Asked about this discrepancy months later, Detective Harper told me, "I missed that. I'll have to listen to it again." By subtly fusing the report in the 911 call of Monday morning texts with later knowledge that the texts were actually a full day earlier, the sheriff contributed to blurring public understanding of the significant fact that WWE had been dealing with a weekend-long crisis, a missing-person case with a long tail. This was one of many examples of fudged facts in the record, which had the cumulative effect of enabling WWE to sell to the public the most sympathetic interpretation of the company's response.

At 1:41 p.m., after the 911 dispatcher told Fagan that the Benoits' front gate was locked and the officers were being deterred by aggressive canines, Fagan expressed surprise, saying, "The message that we got — like I said, he left a message at three o'clock in the morning for another wrestler — 'The gate's open. . . .'" Fagan once again was reinforcing the suggestion that Chris's text message was on Monday rather than Sunday. Fagan also didn't seem to grasp the difference between the main gate to the property and the garage side door leading into the house itself. That would be more understandable, especially if neither Fagan nor anyone else from Andrews International had ever seen the house. But it is another example of, at a minimum, sloppiness in the details.*

In his next call to 911 a half-hour later, at 2:13 p.m., Fagan reported that an unspecified "they" had just gotten back to him with more information. Later he said one of his sources was someone named "Chavo."

"The gentleman I'm dealing with," Fagan said, "is a retired judge in New York." That would be Richard Hering, WWE's vice president of governmental relations and risk management, formerly a justice in upstate Sullivan County. This last piece of trivia could not have been of any interest to the 911 dispatcher. Fagan was trying to impress the listener with his bona fides, or else he was just rambling.

Fagan was now saying he had learned of two separate text messages from Benoit. Actually, Guerrero and Armstrong received a total of at least five texts from Chris in the early morning hours of Sunday.

As for the problem with the dogs in the hour before

---

* Some of the photos of the house plot and individual rooms and evidence, taken by the Crime Scene Unit team and later publicly released, are published in this book. The complete set of those photos is included in the companion disk. See "Order the DVD" at the back of this book.

Holly Schrepfer solved it, Fagan asked, "Can they Taser them — put them to sleep?" *

Fagan checked in twice more with 911, both at times after the Benoit family members had been found dead. Each time, at 3:15 and 4:19, the 911 dispatcher told Fagan that there was not yet any information to impart.

But WWE vice president Hering seemed to be on a more substantive track of communications with the county authorities. At 4:41 Hering called 911 to leave a message for Sheriff's Lieutenant Tommy Pope. Hering said Pope had relayed to Hering a request for certain information in "the Benoit investigation." (Hering did not say if Pope's message had been relayed through Fagan. Perhaps so.) Hering said he had returned Pope's voice messages, but Hering was now calling 911, as well, because he believed Pope was at the house and therefore unable to retrieve the voice messages. **

By the time Fagan, putatively still in the dark, was making his last call to 911, WWE was already deciding to cancel the live wrestling show in Corpus Christi, Texas, and turn that night's edition of *Raw*, the Monday night wrestling show on the USA cable network, into a spontaneously produced three-hour memorial tribute to Chris Benoit. Vince McMahon, the company chairman, was

---

* The dogs' job was to protect Daniel Benoit. Almost certainly, they hopped the backyard fence and roamed the property on their own, because they were hungry and frisky or because they went through the house and saw what had happened. According to a family source, next-door neighbor Holly had made a note to complain to the Benoits about Carny and Highspot's barking on Sunday night.

** The complete audio record of the 911 calls is included in the companion disk. See "Order the DVD" at the back of this book.

explaining all this in a meeting with the wrestlers. By accident or by design, the person who said "I run the security for World Wrestling" was out of the loop — either a well-planted stooge, as clueless as Inspector Clouseau, or playing dumb.*

* * *

Around 3 p.m., Lieutenant Pope and Detective Harper reached the crime scene, directing the activities of a stream of nineteen additional personnel from several agencies who fanned out across the house over the course of the afternoon and evening. At 3:30 a deputy coroner, Bee Huddleston, arrived and made that office's first inspection of the bodies. (In the way of many smaller governments, especially in the American South, Huddleston was also a director of a local funeral home, Carl J. Mowell & Son, whose owner also doubled as the elected county coroner.) Animal control took custody of Carny and Highspot and several kittens cowering in one of the bathrooms.

Detective Bo Turner was put in charge of notifying family. Word of a sensational celebrity crime quickly spread to the public. By 6 p.m. eastern time, WWE had announced on its website:

> World Wrestling Entertainment was informed today by authorities in Fayette County, Ga., that WWE Superstar Chris Benoit, his wife, Nancy, and his son were found dead in their home. Authorities are investigating, but no other details are

---

* Reached by phone on March 27, 2008, Fagan declined to be interviewed, referring all questions to WWE executive Hering, who did not respond to messages.

available at this time.

Instead of its announced programming for tonight on USA Network, WWE will air a three-hour tribute to Chris Benoit.

Chris was beloved among his fellow Superstars, and was a favorite among WWE fans for his unbelievable athleticism and wrestling ability. He always took great pride in his performance, and always showed respect for the business he loved, for his peers and towards his fans. This is a terrible tragedy and an unbearable loss.

WWE extends its sincere condolences and prayers to the surviving members of the Benoit family and their loved ones in this time of tragedy.

The newswire services picked up the item, and wrestling fan sites disseminated it. Leaks of details and speculation flooded blogs, message boards, and chat rooms. Sheriff's officers would blame some of the leaks of early information from the crime scene on District Attorney Scott Ballard, who was already displaying a penchant for loose remarks to whoever pointed a camera at him or held a reporter's notebook.

Fayette County — a placid collection of mostly tony bedroom communities located in the exurbs south of the Atlanta airport — became a center of the media universe. Dozens of television news crews and print reporters, and scores of fans and curiosity-seekers, some traveling vast distances, descended on the scene. Over the next days, Lieutenant Pope and, especially, District Attorney Ballard were regular talking heads on live reports, as the Benoit family tragedy momentarily eclipsed interminable and redundant cable coverage of the most recent misadventures of Britney Spears, Lindsay Lohan, and Paris Hilton.

* * *

Every year in the United States there are scores of domestic homicides — multiple murders of children and the co-heads of households. According to the U.S. Department of Justice, 329 males and 1,181 females were victims of "intimate" homicides in 2005, the most recent year of comprehensive posted statistics by murder category. In the vast majority of multiple-person family homicides, the perpetrator turns out to be the husband-father. A distraught mother is more likely than a father to kill one or more children, but only rarely does the woman murder her spouse as well.

After the most perfunctory confirmation that no one had broken into the Benoit home, no theory for the three deaths other than double murder-suicide by Chris would ever get past first base — for good reason.

Regardless of the circumstances, multiple murder shocks. Doubly disconcerting is the idea that family, the ultimate haven in a heartless world, could also be the logical platform of the ultimate heinous act. This reaction to crime news is an understandable human one, and it applies to families thought to be happy and not; to those known to have domestic violence histories and not; to stories unleashing the homicidal pathology of men from all walks of life, all levels of substance abuse or abstinence, all outward signs of a ticking time bomb or of a heretofore calm exterior.

When the perpetrator is a celebrity, information gets processed through yet another distorting lens. We, the public masses, have acquired a false sense that we share even a glimmer of genuine intimacy with what turns out to be the manufactured image of a real person. We don't readily surrender that illusion.

Here the person was Chris Benoit, the Rabid Wolverine, the Canadian Crippler, the erstwhile masked Pegasus Kid; the embodiment both of fans' thrills and of their denial of the hard truths that enabled those thrills. Fans tend to think in the broad categories of old-time melodramas, populated with heroes and villains — or, as they're known in wrestling, "babyfaces" and "heels." But when Benoit snapped, it was something bigger than a wrestling story line; it was for real, and its awful dimensions made it something akin to wrestling's perfect storm. Occupation-related drug addiction, mental impairment, and lifestyle instability brought into high relief whatever independent personal and marital stressors already existed, and whatever predisposition Benoit might already have carried for resolving in the worst way his inner turmoil.

In the perfect storm, Benoit was the perfect vessel. He linked wrestling's past with wrestling's future, its small-time regional roots with its corporate global reach. Trading in the possibility of a developed private life, he pursued a distinguished public career, but one that in the end was fatally tarnished.

CHAPTER 2

Chris & Nancy

STAR-CROSSED WRESTLING LOVERS, Chris Benoit and Nancy Toffoloni were born on the same day, May 21 — he in 1967, she three years earlier. He was the wrestler's wrestler, the living, breathing descendent of the style of Tom Billington, the legendary "Dynamite Kid." She was a breakthrough figure in the sexualization of wrestling's femme fatales, so prototypical in portraying the charms and treacheries of a woman that her last character was known — with an efficiency as stunning as her physical beauty — simply as "Woman."

Born in Montreal, Chris moved with his family to Edmonton at a young age. It is no exaggeration to note that he never knew any life outside wrestling. Captivated by the televised shows of Stampede Wrestling, Stu Hart's Western Canada territory, Benoit began turning up at Stampede shows as early as age eleven, volunteering to set up and tear down the folding chairs for ringside seating at Edmonton's Kinsmen Field House.

In 1980, at thirteen, Chris engineered a backstage meeting with the Dynamite Kid, his favorite wrestler. The British Kid, then in his early twenties, was already the lead bad guy for Stampede and an industry revolutionary. In Japan with Satoru Sayama, "Tiger Mask," Tom Billington broke new ground in the working of matches. His bouts were built around highspots and lightning-quick changes of advantage. So spectacular were the Kid's athletic precision, timing, and psychology that they obliterated conventional notions of lifting the crowd's emotions slowly up and down; the Kid kept everyone in a bell-to-bell frenzy. With his cousin Davey Boy Smith, he would graduate from Stampede to a lucrative run in the World Wrestling Federation (wwf, later wwe) as the British Bulldogs tag team.

In order to get there, Billington had to take thousands of bumps in rings before smaller audiences, and he lived on the painkillers and alcohol that got him through the physical and mental ordeal. He also gassed himself to the gills on steroids, because if a small man could find a small opening in the big time, it was still just a small opening, and you still needed to meet a minimum size threshold. In 1986 he had spinal surgery. The next year he had the first of two near-fatal seizures. By 1996, at thirty-seven, he was through for good, though he had been a shell of the classic Dynamite Kid for many years, messed up by injuries and by a menu of drugs that included both lsd and gammahydroxybutyrate or gbh, popularly known as the "date-rape drug." Divorced from wrestling great Bret Hart's sister-in-law, and from a second wife, Billington returned to England to live alone, in a wheel-chair, and on the dole.

In 1980, all thirteen-year-old Chris Benoit knew was that he wanted to be exactly like the Dynamite Kid. Chris begged his family to get him weight-training equipment, and his father complied. Scrawny but determined, he lifted enough and took enough steroids to pump himself over the 200-pound mark (he would grow to a little over five-eight, quite short for a star wrestler, and weigh around 220, sometimes more, at the peak of his career).

When he was eighteen, Chris knocked on Stu Hart's door in Calgary and asked for a tryout with Stampede. Stu did what he first did with all wannabes: he took Chris down to the Hart house basement gym, known as the Dungeon, where the upstart was stretched and "hooked" in numerous vein-bursting, impossible-to-break legitimate wrestling holds. It was certifiable torture. Benoit passed the test by not complaining that day and by returning for more the next day, and he was put into the rotation for full training as a pro wrestler. He learned how to distribute his body to cushion those jarring bumps to the extent possible. He learned how to "sell" an opponent's moves, how to carry himself, how to play off his opponent. These were in weekend sessions; at that time, Chris worked for his dad's business in Edmonton during the week and made the nearly 200-mile commute to Calgary by bus every Friday, returning home Sunday evening.

Later in '85, Stampede sent Benoit out on tour in wrestling's exalted backwater, the often frozen tundra of the Western Canadian prairie. Every week the boys drove from Calgary to Saskatoon, Regina, Red Deer, and Edmonton, in a four-wheel-drive van prone to breaking down in the middle of nowhere. And Chris loved it, and the fans loved him. They said he was the spitting image of the Dynamite Kid — the same dives without regard for his own neck, even the same crisply executed snap suplexes.

In 1987, Benoit moved to Japan to live for a year in the dojo, or training facility, of one of the two top promotions there, New Japan Pro Wrestling. The punishment could hardly exceed what he had already experienced in the Dungeon. But dojos also boasted strict pecking orders and hazing rituals, and for a foreign peon, the psychological humiliations were even worse. Chris did the dirtiest housekeeping chores and ran the most degrading errands for the veterans, all while picking up more tricks of the trade, Japanese style. Eventually New Japan booked him as the masked Pegasus Kid, and he was formidable enough in that role to capture championships and become a two-time winner of the Super J Cup, a prestigious tournament dedicated to the junior heavyweight division.

Benoit also wrestled in Mexico and Europe. Working in the German "catch" league, he met his first wife, Martina, with whom he would have a son and a daughter in Edmonton before divorcing. In Japan, where the master German wrestler Karl Gotch was a major influence, Chris already had perfected, and made into one of his patented moves, the German suplex, in which his opponent was whiplashed up and over Benoit's body and onto his own neck.

They called Benoit "The Rabid Wolverine." While at the Philadelphia-based Extreme Championship Wrestling in 1994, Benoit cemented a second nickname: "The Canadian Crippler." This came after he accidentally broke the neck of another wrestler, Sabu, when they miscommunicated and botched a move. Promoters rarely miss an opportunity to exploit even unintended doses of reality, and ECW's Paul Heyman was no exception. Under Heyman's tutelage, ECW generally upped the ante on violence and risk. Marketing largely to young kids in the early Hulk Hogan years, WWF had taken on a comparatively patterned and safe style. But the promotional war with World Championship Wrestling (wcw), Ted Turner's Atlanta promotion, along with ecw's way-out-there rendition of the art of the work, pushed wwf to enhance its athleticism and cater more to a demanding new base of "hardcore" fans. Though more often playing a babyface than a heel, Benoit embraced the elevation of his persona to that of a ruthless dispenser of spinal injuries. His submission finishing hold was called the Crippler Crossface.

Chris, who had wrestled briefly for wcw in 1993, returned permanently, with a nice guaranteed contract, in 1995. At twenty-eight, in his athletic prime, he finally had a foothold in the North American wrestling mainstream.

* * *

Like Chris, Nancy Toffoloni had started in wrestling as a fan, hooked up with a regional troupe in the territorial days, and risen to a steady position with one of the two major companies left standing in the cable TV era.

Nancy graduated from high school in DeLand, Florida, near Daytona Beach. She got a job selling programs at the Orlando shows of Championship Wrestling, a promotion based in Tampa, and owned and operated by former wrestler Eddie Graham. The Graham office, which controlled all of Florida, was one of the most successful of what at one time were more than thirty thriving full-time regional promotions throughout the United States. Graham had a tight relationship with the largest line of independent pulp wrestling magazines published in New York. A photographer for the magazines discovered Nancy and used her first as a bikini model and then in a series of pictorials, popular at the time, that were billed as "apartment house wrestling." These were soft-core porn depictions, catering to the fantasies of young men and boys, of attractive women groping each other in street clothes, which were often shed in stages in the midst of matches said to be privately staged for an exclusive clientele. They weren't wrestling bouts at all, of course, just cheesy still photo shoots. Apartment house wrestling stories sold well on newsstands and were credited with extending the heyday of the by-then-struggling old-school wrestling mags.

Playing the apartment house girl named Para, Nancy met wrestler Kevin Sullivan at one of the sessions. Nearly fifteen years older, the stumpy Bostonian was taken by her youthful curves and her sultry dark features, which included prominent cheekbones and eyes that narrowed menacingly on cue. In 1984, at age twenty, she began touring with Sullivan on the Florida wrestling circuit as his valet. "Fallen Angel" was also mixed up in the TV character Sullivan created for himself, the "Prince of Darkness," some sort of satanic cult guru, in a story line considered innovative for its time. Nancy had married Jim Daus, a boyfriend from DeLand, but she soon divorced him and married Sullivan.

With the exception of a few gimmick matches, Nancy didn't wrestle. Yet as one of the most "over" of the '80s generation of valets or managers, she helped pivot the participation of females in pro wrestling away from their burlesque-like and largely unglamorous roots. In the golden age, most were trained in the tired formulas of promoter Billy Wolfe and, later, long-time champion Lillian Ellison ("The Fabulous Moolah"); they wore one-piece suits and mixed a few moves of mat grappling with mild elements of catfights and gender-based sight gags. (In Moolah's favorite heel spot, she hid a "foreign object" in her brassiere and was never busted because the referee "couldn't" inspect there.) Following Nancy Sullivan and her contemporaries were today's fitness-queen vixens, the WWE divas, who mostly drive website traffic and push merchandise, as well as tangle on the undercards of live shows.

Championship Wrestling from Florida folded during the promotional war fueled by Vince McMahon's national expansion of the WWF. Kevin and Nancy, however, landed on their feet with the cast of WCW. Sullivan became influential on the WCW booking committee, and Nancy stayed on the air as Woman, a manager with assorted protégés and story lines. With one significant break for a run by the Sullivans together, and then separately, in Extreme Championship Wrestling, that was where things stood when Chris Benoit got his own permanent WCW gig.

What happened next was a milestone moment in wrestling's seemingly boundless capacity for life imitating art. Kevin and Nancy's marriage, tumultuous all along, was on its last legs. Meanwhile, Sullivan, wearing the hat of booker, noticed that Benoit, a brilliant but colorless performer, could use an "angle" that gave him more "heat" and drawing power. And maybe Chris and Nancy also had eyes for each other, really and truly and almost instantly. Only their hairdressers knew.

Whatever the bottom line in reality, Chris and Nancy were thrown together in TV skits in which they messed around behind Kevin's back, and sometimes right in front of him. This kindled a wrestling feud between Benoit and Sullivan, culminating in a match that Chris won with the stipulation that Kevin then had to "retire." (In fact, Sullivan was plotting his retreat from the ring to concentrate full-time on wcw management.) Nancy soon formally left Kevin and moved in with Chris. The inside joke in the industry was that Sullivan was the booker who had scripted his own divorce.

Further complicating the picture was wcw's subsequent puzzling refusal to push Benoit harder as a main-event attraction. That may have been personal retribution on Sullivan's part, or it may simply have been yet another reflection of the company's wall-to-wall mismanagement. By this time, several other smaller wrestlers were in the same boat, including Benoit's pals Eddie Guerrero and Dean Malenko, who were also undersized but talented; they called themselves the "Three Amigos." All were wooed by wwf and jumped. Benoit's case for release from his high-paying but frustrating wcw contract was strengthened when the Turner human resources department learned that Mike Graham, one of Sullivan's assistants, had threatened to slit Chris's throat. (Graham was the son of Nancy's Florida boss, Eddie Graham, who committed suicide in 1985.) Chris took a pay cut to leave Georgia for Connecticut, but he was happy to abandon, after only a single day, the wcw championship that was belatedly bestowed on him. Long-term, this proved an excellent career move.

Weeks after debuting with wwf early in 2000, Chris was given a few days off to join Nancy in Georgia as she gave birth to their son, Daniel Christopher Benoit, on February 25. Chris and Nancy married nine months later.

* * *

In 2003, Chris's wrestling home, which had changed its name to WWE, embarked on a public education program to tame a phenomenon the media were labeling "backyard wrestling," in which anecdotes emerged of serious injury and even death. In the 1950s, several kids were reported to have jumped from upper-story windows trying to emulate actor George Reeves in the TV series *Superman*, which led the show's producers to insert into scripts disclaimers about how no mortal should ever attempt the feats Superman performed. Similarly, WWE bowed to pressure in its "Don't try this" warnings to young viewers at home. The company cooperated with the Canada Safety Council in a campaign that included an appearance by Benoit on *Canada AM*. The host, Ravi Bachwal, showed a video clip of Benoit executing the Crippler Crossface and asked him to explain it.

"Basically, this is a submission move where I'll ride the guy down by his arm and wrap my hands and lock my hands around his face," Benoit said. "And I pull back as hard as I can on his head. It is really a devastating submission move when applied correctly. But you get a lot of these kids in the backyard that watch us doing it, and have no training, no experience, do not have any idea of how to apply the hold."

"Among kids, what could they do to each other if they tried this move?" Bachwal asked.

"Oh, you could tear a rotator cuff. You could dislocate your shoulder. Severe nerve damage, spinal damage."

WWE put up a website with advice for parents. An article in *WWE Magazine* showed how Benoit did the Crippler Crossface, "arguably the most feared submission hold in the sport":

> As the head is pulled back, the victim's neck is at a point of severe stress [and] the carotid arteries and the jugular veins are partially cut off, depriving the brain of precious blood. . . . [W]ith Benoit's hands clasped across his opponent's face, the possibility of a broken nose is very real.

* * *

WrestleMania XX, March 14, 2004. A packed Madison Square Garden in New York and an international pay-per-view audience watched the main event, a "Triple Threat Match" in which Benoit and Shawn Michaels simultaneously challenged Triple H for the WWE Raw brand's world heavyweight championship.

Twenty-four minutes into the brutal three-way ballet, Michaels launched his finishing move, the superkick he called Sweet Chin Music. Benoit ducked and Michaels went flying out of the ring.

Attacking Benoit from behind, Triple H attempted his coup de grace, a face-first piledriver called the Pedigree. But the Rabid Wolverine spun out and reversed it, clamping Triple H in his own finisher, the Crippler Crossface. Triple H reached for the ropes to force a break, but Benoit managed to roll him back to the center of the ring, and the champion had to tap out.

After fighting for eighteen years in hundreds of venues, large and small, on three continents, Chris Benoit was a champion of wrestling's only truly worldwide franchise. As the belt was handed to him, Benoit's face contorted in pain, joy, and awe. Eddie Guerrero — who earlier on the show had successfully defended the WWE championship, the top title of WWE's SmackDown brand — entered the ring. The two best friends embraced tearfully.

Chris's dad, Mike Benoit, and Chris's son and daughter from his first marriage, David and Megan, had flown in for the show, and they climbed through the ropes and joined the celebration. So did Nancy and Daniel (who had recently turned four). Confetti fell from the rafters. They hugged. They cried.

* * *

The first pay-per-view after *WrestleMania XX* was *Backlash*, from Edmonton's Rexall Place. WWE orchestrated a five-day buildup centered around the local kid who made good. Thousands of fans greeted Benoit at a rally when he arrived at Edmonton International Airport on Tuesday, April 13, 2004. Mayor Bill Smith declared Sunday "Chris Benoit Day."

"Excitement is building," Mayor Smith said in a WWE news release, "as local wrestling fans prepare to welcome their hometown hero for Backlash® on April 18. It will be a great time in Edmonton."

CHAPTER 3

Living with Death

ON NOVEMBER 13, 2005, Chavo Guerrero found his uncle and fellow wrestler, Eddie Guerrero, thirty-eight years old, unconscious on the bathroom floor of his room at the Marriott City Center Hotel in Minneapolis. By the time Chavo carried Eddie to the bed and performed CPR, he was probably already dead of a heart attack.

Chavo called Chris Benoit, who arrived quickly. Before calling 911, Chavo and Chris took care of an important preliminary piece of business: they flushed down the toilet Eddie's supply of stanozolol (Winstrol), an anabolic steroid he'd just stocked up on for an upcoming European tour. In 1984, in a hotel room in Tokyo, Bruiser Brody flushed away David Von Erich's Placidyl sleeping pills before the authorities arrived. Ever since, concealing the drugs near a dead wrestler was standard operating procedure for colleagues interested in protecting the business.

WWE would explain Eddie Guerrero's fatal coronary as a consequence of his "past" abuse of alcohol and non-steroid drugs during his time with another promotion, before his very public and inspiring rehabilitation with

WWE. The grim truth, however, was that Eddie was "clean" only in wrestlers' vernacular; he could not have maintained the size required to perform in his main-event-level push while being truly free of steroids. "Clean" here means not that he didn't use but that he, allegedly, didn't abuse.*

Five months younger than Chris Benoit, Eddie Guerrero was his soul mate. Both were superb technicians who climbed improbably to the pinnacle of their profession without the advantage of great size. Guerrero descended from a famous Mexican wrestling family, and his fast-paced, high-flying style (derived in part from the *lucha libre* tradition) fit awkwardly with the ponderous big-man choreography of the major U.S. promotions, especially WWE's. But the steroid scandals of the 1990s had created a bit of daylight for diversity in the size of the top wrestling talent, as an acrobatic masked wrestler, Rey Mysterio, proved that a smaller man could get "over" in the major leagues. Though not the high flier that Mysterio was, Guerrero led a savvy pack, combining ring generalship with a refined grasp of crowd psychology. Like Benoit and their "Three Amigos" running mate, Dean Malenko (another second-generation wrestler), Guerrero had honed his craft by synthesizing techniques picked up not only on the American indie circuit but also in extensive tours of the wrestling-mad capitals of Japan and Mexico.

That Guerrero and Benoit could survive the orthopedic punishment of wrestling, combined with the

---

* Sixteen months after Guerrero's death and three months before Benoit's, the former would be named in an investigation of steroids in sports published on the *Sports Illustrated* website.

indignities visited upon them by promoters who under-appreciated and mishandled them, was a triumph of will. That they both could go on to achieve out-and-out superstardom in the face of these odds approached the miraculous. And indeed, spirituality became an openly expressed facet of Eddie's public persona. He was simultaneously tough and tender, macho and sensitive, vulnerable and unsinkable. He projected himself as the representation of the common man — and the common fan. To boot, he was a recovering alcoholic who gave witness to a higher power.

Like Benoit, Guerrero was a world-class worker inside the ring. Unlike Benoit, Guerrero also wove sharp interviews and story lines outside it. In February 2004, Guerrero won a WWE world title the month before Benoit won his at *WrestleMania*. At the time of his death, Guerrero was arguably the company's most charismatic performer.

In televised tributes to Guerrero on special TV episodes of *Raw* and *SmackDown*, WWE cast members broke character, pouring out their genuine and unanimous affection. No testimonial was as searing as Benoit's. He could barely get his words out through sobs and wails of grief:

> Eddie Guerrero was my best friend, and I'm sure there's a lot of people he knew that would be able to say the same thing about him. He was such a beautiful person, such a kind-hearted person. I couldn't find the words — words couldn't describe — what kind of human being Eddie truly was. I've known Eddie for just about fifteen years and spent a good portion of the fifteen years with him on the road. We laughed together, cried together, fought each other, been up and down each and every

mountain, each and every highway. Eddie always led by example. He was the one friend I could go to and pour my heart out to, if I was going through something, if I had a personal issue, a personal problem, he was the one guy I could call and talk to and know that he would understand, and he would talk me out of it, because of all the experiences he'd been through. I believe in leading by example, and Eddie always led by example through his life, because of all the obstacles he went through and conquered and became a better person, and he often used that as an example. We never left each other without telling each other that we loved each other, and I truly can say that I love Eddie Guerrero. He's a man that I can say I love, and I love his family, and my heart and my thoughts and my prayers go out to. And Eddie, I know that you're in a better place. I know that you're looking down on me right now. I only know that I love you and I miss you. *[Pause as Benoit breaks down completely.]* Eddie, you made such a great impression on my life, and I want to thank you for everything you've ever given me, and I want to thank you from my heart and tell you that I love you and I'll never forget you, and that we'll see each other again. I love you, Eddie.

At that point, Guerrero was the highest-level active wrestling star to drop dead. The industry's mortality rate was accelerating; now it was even losing its locker room leaders. Chris Benoit watched helplessly as his personal mentors, confidantes, and surrogate family went to early graves, one by one.

On January 28, 2006, Victor Mar Manuel, the Mexican wrestler known as "Black Cat" who had trained Benoit in Japan, died of a heart attack. Manuel was 51.

Nineteen days later, Penny Dunham found the lifeless body of her husband Michael, the ex-wrestler known as "Johnny Grunge," in bed at their home in Peachtree City,

Georgia. Mike Dunham was thirty-nine. The cause of death cited — complications from sleep apnea, or airway blockage — rarely told the whole story. Dunham was morbidly obese. He had ingested a huge quantity of Soma pills, muscle relaxers prescribed by Phil Astin, the same doctor who treated Benoit.

Four years earlier, Johnny Grunge's old partner in the tag team Public Enemy, Theodore Petty ("Rocco Rock"), had died at forty-nine.

Dunham was Benoit's last link to his original circle of wrestling friends in the Atlanta area. Though estranged from most of the others, Chris had kept up with Johnny, and Nancy with Penny. On top of the loss of Guerrero, Grunge was the one that broke Chris. He no longer felt that he had anyone with whom he could talk intimately.

Though he continued to devote himself to performing to the highest standards, his fortieth birthday was approaching and his in-ring skills were diminishing. The phenomenon was subtle — nothing his superior experience and psychology couldn't cover for several or even many more years — but the joy of the process had abandoned him. One's position in the pecking order of the promotion was just one part of the payoff for all those one-night stands, all that pain. To keep from becoming unglued, you also needed an inchoate but ever-present sense of camaraderie: the banter, the ribs or practical jokes, all the absurdities that, amidst the pressure and the mindfucking, provided detachment and pleasure.

Even Eddie Guerrero's sudden passing, in a strange room on the road at the height of his powers, carried a note of elegy in the denouement of a tragic life. But Johnny Grunge's decay was simply sordid, coldly judgmental on the shallow resources of Chris's limited world.

As wrestlers died, a new and macabre subgenre emerged: memorial benefit shows. Most prominently, from 1998 through 2001, Cincinnati promoter Les Thatcher ran an annual production to assist the widow and children of Brian Pillman, who had wrestled with Benoit at Stampede and died suddenly at thirty-five while with WWF. Benoit (along with Eddie Guerrero, Rey Mysterio, and Konnan, a Cuban-born star in Mexico and on the U.S. independent scene) was known as one of the most generous of the top-tier wrestlers; on his days off, he volunteered for the Pillman and other benefits.

The Pillman show on May 25, 2000, at the Schmidt Fieldhouse on the Xavier University campus, featured a classic match between Benoit and William Regal. The exhibition, memorable for its realistic butchery, was credited with reviving Regal's career and spurring WWE to sign him shortly thereafter. WWE had permitted Thatcher to bill the match as being for the WWE inter-continental championship, one of the company's minor titles, and the end product was impressive enough that the video of it would be included in a DVD package of Benoit highlights entitled *Hard Knocks*.

Dave Meltzer of the *Wrestling Observer Newsletter*, who was in Cincinnati that night, remembered it as "the same Benoit-Regal match they always did," with a spot in which they head-butted each other repeatedly until they drew so-called "hardway" blood. In other words, rather than concealing razor blades inside their wrist bands before pulling them out and discreetly scraping them over scar tissue on their foreheads — the conventional method of "juicing" — Benoit and Regal legitimately pounded on, or "potatoed," each other until the red stuff gushed, whipping the crowd into a froth.

"I don't think there were any specific instructions other than Regal wanted the best match possible, as they had done that spot in matches before and they did it in matches after," Meltzer said. "This one is remembered because of the setting and because they were given time instead of being rushed through. Regal credits it for saving his career when everyone wrote him off for his ongoing drug problems. He's a friend of Triple H [Vince McMahon's son-in-law], so who's to say Regal wouldn't have gotten the chance anyway, but it's not an exaggeration to say that he revived his reputation with this match, and it likely saved his career at that time."

After Guerrero and then Grunge joined the long list of fatalities, Chris had had it. He swore off benefit shows — and funerals. They were too depressing.

CHAPTER 4

Last Days in Fayette County

IN THE SUMMER OF 2006, Holly Schrepfer was driving home when she saw a disheveled and upset woman walking along Quarters Road. The woman was her new next-door neighbor, Nancy Benoit, whom Holly had not yet properly met. Holly asked Nancy if she was OK. The answer was no, not exactly — she had just had a fight with her husband, who threw her against the wall, and she was afraid to go back inside. Holly drove Nancy to a hotel near the Atlanta airport, where she spent a couple of nights before things at home cooled off.

In the first years of their marriage, the Benoits, employed by the Atlanta-based WCW, had settled in Peachtree City. Wrestlers from the South generally liked to live closer to the center of metropolitan Atlanta. Outsiders like Benoit (Canada), Johnny Grunge (New Jersey), William Regal (Great Britain), and Fit Finlay (Ireland) favored Peachtree, another rim away from the nearest suburbs and somewhat more sanitized, even sensory-deprived. WCW ring announcer Dave Penzer and TV cameraman Darwin Conort also lived there. The wrestling people formed a regular social circle, hanging out together at places like the Ginza Japanese Steak House. Their wives, especially, bonded, swapping insecure gossip about what their husbands were up to on the road.

But eventually the Benoits withdrew from the group. Chris, who could be gregarious on the road, was distant and awkward at home. The only person with whom he continued to keep in touch was Grunge, which was why his death, on top of Eddie's, hit Chris so hard.

The core of Benoit's personality remained an enigma to the end. Even some of his closest friends and colleagues could be intimidated by his intensity, his single-minded focus on wrestling, and his fanatical workout regime of stair-climbing and squats, along with weight training, from which he had never lapsed, going all the way back to his days of humiliation at the lowest level at a Japanese dojo. Former wrestler Superstar Billy Graham was among those who observed a fundamental social disconnect, a quality whereby Benoit, in the middle of a non-wrestling dialogue in a group situation, was prone to zoning out without warning. Later, struggling to make sense of Chris's murderous rampage, Graham remembered that a lot of the guys called Benoit "the zombie."

Another wrestling colleague who puzzled over Benoit was Chris Masters, who put it this way: "To be perfectly honest, I respected the hell out of Chris Benoit for being the man that he was, but there was always an intense energy coming from him every time I shook his hand. It made for sometimes short and awkward conversations."

On CNN's *Nancy Grace*, fellow Canadian wrestler Chris Jericho described Benoit as "almost a tale of two cities, a tale of two people. There is the Chris Benoit that had these horrendous acts of extreme psychopathic lunacy in the last couple days of his life, and then there's the Benoit that I myself traveled with, lived with, said 'I love you' to on many occasions. He was my mentor. He was one of my best friends. And he was a brother to me in so many ways. And the fifteen years I knew him and the two days that he decided to do these horrible, horrible acts, it's hard to kind of discern the two. And that's why we have to figure out what would cause such a mild-mannered, polite, influential, tremendous person and performer to do such things."

Jericho called Benoit "a very quiet man but not a recluse and not a hermit, just quiet. He minded his own business, but he was always around. If there was a joke, he would laugh. And of all the years I was with him, I never once saw anything — if there was a fight — if I went nuts and wanted to beat somebody up, he was the guy that would contain me. And a lot of people can tell you that."

Journalist Dave Meltzer also had a nuanced view of Benoit. He considered being accessible to his fans his own important responsibility, and when Meltzer launched an Internet radio show in 1999, Benoit was his first on-air guest. "Chris was uncomfortable and distant, but was very nice and a good listener to those he knew," Meltzer said. "I think he was someone who was always thinking and a very private person. He definitely needed to be by himself and didn't like being social at times. He internalized a lot. He was *not* a 'dumb jock' type."

One factor in Chris and Nancy's isolation from the Peachtree City circle was that, even back then, they had a habit of breaking out in operatic public fights that embarrassed those around them. Nancy had a sharp tongue, especially when she was boozed or pilled up, and she hit all of Chris's buttons. Their friends were hardly surprised when, in June 2003, Nancy filed for divorce and was granted a temporary restraining order based on an April incident in which Chris, according to Nancy's court papers, "lost his temper and threatened to strike the petitioner and cause extensive damage to the home and personal belongings of the parties, including furniture." In August, they reconciled and Chris moved back in.

* * *

If Chris wasn't a hermit before he lost his twin anchors of Eddie Guerrero and Johnny Grunge, he became one afterwards. The Benoits built a sprawling new house, in the classic Federal style, at the edge of Fayetteville. They didn't even bother to secure a purchaser for the Peachtree house before moving to the new one — partly because the housing market was in a slump and they didn't need the cash, and partly because Chris wanted nothing more than to wall himself off in a gated mansion, as quickly as possible.

In addition to eschewing wrestlers' funerals, Chris renounced religion. Or maybe he swore by it as much as at it — the distinction wasn't clear. Nancy took him to counseling sessions with their pastor, George Dillard of the Peachtree City Christian Church. Together, husband and wife read the Bible, and he started memorizing passages, which he quoted to friends and family.

Chris's remarks in an email to journalist Greg Oliver shortly after Guerrero's death showed the unrealized objectives of a tortured odyssey:

I know that he has left us but I still feel like I'm going to see him on the road next week. I do not know if I will ever have as good a friend as I did in Eddie. I was able to talk to him about anything in my life, and he was always able to make sense of things or change my perspective.

He was somewhat of a spiritual guide for me. I do not know if you read the Bible at all, or what your beliefs are, and I will respect you for whatever your beliefs are. But if you ever get the opportunity to read about Job, it reminds me so much of Eddie. At one point after coming out of rehab, he had nothing but the clothes on his back. He had physically, mentally, emotionally and monetarily hit rock bottom. He lost his family; his wife and children had left. But he never lost his faith and through it was able to overcome the odds.

Instead of Eddie becoming bitter, Eddie became better. In our business it is really difficult to understand why we do what we do and why we think what we think unless you are in it, unless you have a passion for it. It is so demanding physically, mentally and emotionally in every possible way, but when you love it as did Eddie, as I do, you have a better understanding of why we do what we do.

I do not believe that I will ever find someone that I will bond with and be able to understand and be understood as I was with Eddie. I'm not looking forward to going back on the road, not that I ever did. I hate the road, but I looked forward to Eddie's company and camaraderie. Both of us hated the road, being away from our families, but both of us lived for that in-ring bell-to-bell time.

Without his Three Amigos road partner, Chris was lonelier than ever, but this condition collided with an ironic reality: while the WWE schedule remained punishing, it was somewhat more manageable than it used to be. The war with WCW was long over, and WWE talent no longer needed to be away from their families 300 days a year. Live events were built more than ever around TV shoots and pay-per-views; though there were still regular "house" shows, as well, the scheduling was marginally lighter and more rational. In December 2005, while Nancy recuperated from surgery in which a long-damaged disk in her neck was fused and repaired, the company even gave Chris an extended leave, which also gave him a chance to recover from several nagging injuries.

But even if you could afford the expenses of bouncing back and forth from the road to home (and Chris, who made more than $500,000 a year, could afford it more than most), you had to make choices, and Chris was increasingly choosing to stay away. Like many wrestlers, he liked to say he was a homebody at heart, and like many wrestlers, he seemed to be saying so, with repetition and overwrought sentiment, in an effort to convince himself as much as others. "Quality time with my family is a big vice. It's something I'll fight for and crave," he told the *Calgary Sun* in 2004.

The juxtapositions — "quality time," "vice," "crave" — showed an inconsistency of more than just rhetoric. The evidence of the last months of Chris and Nancy's lives, including an incomplete record of the text messages from their cell phones, brings into high relief the bitterness of their alienation, spotlighting both specific issues and the general inability of this particular man, in a profession celebrating misogny, to embrace domesticity.

In late March 2007, Nancy told her mother-in-law that she suspected Chris was not "doing the right thing" on the road. Margaret Benoit said she would talk to Chris about it on his July trip to Canada.

On May 5, Nancy text-messaged Chris: *"Daniel has called twice today. What you cant bother with him either."*

On the morning of May 9: *"One night your textgng I love you durin the day you wont talk. Get off the crap your on its makin you passive aggressive and I dont need the abuse."*

Three hours later, the subject was Nancy's charge that Chris had not made himself available to his two kids with Martina, who were visiting from Canada: *"Your big claim ask anyone you work with how you are, know one knows what goes on behind closed doors. and the excuses about not being able to see your kids is your failure in putting no effort to them. paying out lots of money sending for them twice a year is a far cry for being a Dad. you need to get it together. I will not except this steroid enduced roller-coaster ride of emotional abuse. ignoring the problem or running away isnt going to help you face it you need professional and only if your fully honest about all of it."*

That afternoon: *"You don't get it I do not except your emotional and verbal abuse. you want to talk to me your gonna have to put more effort into it than this."*

The next day: *"You are a grown man with three kids set the example are you trying to say this is how you grew up watching your dad call your mom names and make her cry? No then what gives you the right! grow up for mighty sakes get off the stuff its obvious im probably not the only one who can see and we both know the [WWE] wellness program is a joke."*

On the morning of May 12: *"I tried to put an end to*

this your the one who is draging it out its stupid you could have been home last your doing."

That afternoon: *"Daniel has been calling you you need to call him and me too this has gone on long enough i tried to talk to you you could have been at home yesterday."*

That night: *"If you havent figure daniel knows how to dial your cell by pushing phonebook and scrolling to 'chris cell' hes mad at me cause you havent called be an adult and call. It wont take much more for him to realize its not me hes mad at hes not a baby any more and a message isnt going to be enough."*

May 22, ex-wife and in-law problems: *"The german christmas ornament would not have bothered me had* [Martina] *not kept asking about it especially when she kept asking about it on my birthday, she tried to ignore me on Mothers Day I called back twice. So when your parents do come I will confront your mom she has put me in the middle this time. I'll handle it. Ten years now, havent been here and now still cant come when the Kids are together. My folks are coming just for the Kids summer holiday. Effort. second on my list to Help. We asked when I had the big surgery. Two years ago. It's enough already. No more excuses just be real!"*

On May 26, Nancy seemed to be mocking Chris's complaint that his hard work was not appreciated by his dependents: *"Money orders every month cant give hugs. you should keep working wouldnt want the ex to miss another four weeks paid while you send for your annual Im a great father summer holiday!"* And: *"What's sixty thousand times ten? six hundred thousand. boy, I feel sorry for you, all that money, time and effort and still no thank you, no thanks for the trips every year, twice, three times at least a year. I wonder does anyone really know when they go to bed at night or eat a meal or wear the clothes they put on how tired you are at the end week or how very very hard it is to work for six hundred thousand. nope, its much easier to have it handed to you with four weeks paid holiday. yuo. no idea what you've lost. no need to worry Ill make sure your sacrifices are well know."*

In another text later that day, Nancy zeroed in on the apparent heart of the matter: Chris's refusal to change the beneficiaries on an old $250,000 life insurance policy, which still listed as beneficiaries Martina and their children: *"If you wanted your exwife to have your retirement fund you would have given to her ten years ago at the divorce. If you wanted her to have more you wouldn't have tried to hide your money. Now it's the point, we are married. I come first."*

* * *

Nancy told her neighbor Holly that the stress of it all had led her to abuse alcohol and prescription medications. Trying to hold things together for Daniel, she began taking long walks to get into better physical condition, and she vowed to cut back on her drinking. But it was hard. Even when Chris was coming home between shows, instead of staying on the road, he was "emotionally detached," Nancy said.

In this account, Chris was also controlling: he didn't want his wife to have friends or a means of transportation. After one fight, Chris hid her Hummer. Holly had to drive Nancy around the airport parking facilities until they found it. Chris would try to micromanage her from the road — for example, he would call home and tell her exactly what to cook that night.

In March 2007, while Chris's son David and daughter Megan were visiting from Canada for a week, Chris and Nancy fought loudly on several occasions. At least once, Nancy pushed and hit Chris. (Nancy was furious that, among other things, Chris had made no preparation or plans for time with his older children.) After that fight, David left the house with Chris and they had dinner out. At other times, David took little Daniel upstairs to shield him from what was going on.

Finally, there were the drugs. Chris had abused steroids for decades, to the point where his own endocrine system had stopped producing its own normal supply of testosterone. This became the basis for a therapeutic use exemption under the WWE wellness program; with a doctor's prescription, he could continue to inject testosterone and other steroids under the guise of "testosterone replacement therapy." Nancy may have been frustrated by his impaired sexual function, which limited his performance in the bedroom during his less-and-less frequent time at home.

In general, she was concerned about what she termed Chris's "bee-stinging," or the heavy amounts of steroids he shot up. In the case of his painkillers and mood drugs, Nancy occasionally appropriated them for herself. In the case of the steroids, at least once — in late January 2007 — she threw out a stash. Chris was so angry about this that he left home for two weeks.

In May, wrestler Bob Howard ("Hardcore Holly") would tell the sheriff's investigators, Chris checked into a local hotel after a fight. Chris said Nancy was "fucked up" on pills and booze.

* * *

On June 14, Chris had this text exchange with fellow wrestler Gregory ("Hurricane") Helms:

(Benoit) *How many men does it take to open a bottle of beer? — none it should already be open when the bitch brings it.*

(Benoit) *How are women and toilet bowls similar? — If the hole in the middle isnt worth a shit.*

(Helms) *Or how is a woman's pussy like a warm toilet seat? — They both feel nice but u can't help but wonder who was there before you!*

CHAPTER 5

The Lost Weekend

ON SATURDAY, JUNE 16, Chris Benoit wrestled in Dothan, Alabama, 200 miles south of Fayetteville. Nancy joined him at the show. Her suspicions that Chris was having an affair deepened. Backstage, it seemed to her that WWE people were walking on eggshells around her, as if everyone else knew something she didn't.

Inside WWE, the rumor was that Benoit was, indeed, having an affair with diva Michelle McCool, a blonde bombshell former schoolteacher who, coincidentally, hailed from the same northern Florida region as Nancy. The sheriff's log of text messages would show that on November 30, 2006, Chris asked another wrestler, "Could you please text me Michelle McCools number please?"

Also on the log are redactions of the phone number or numbers (represented only as "xxx-xxx-xxxx," perhaps to protect privacy) to which Benoit texted about his arrivals on Delta Airlines flights in May 2007. Chris was telling the recipient that he would arrive at 9:32 a.m. on May 3 and at 8:25 a.m. on May 5. (In between, on May 4, Chris appeared to have made a one-day hop home.) Verizon

Wireless produced crude printouts of all the call information from the Benoits' phones, but the data starts on June 1; therefore, it's impossible to determine to whom those two texts were directed. Thursday, May 3, was a company off-day, so if Chris was conducting any business, it would have been a non-wrestling promotional appearance. Saturday, May 5, was the date of two WWE shows in Poughkeepsie, New York. McCool, like Benoit, was booked in both of them.

(McCool did not respond to requests for comment sent through the contact emails on her website. The wrestler from whom Benoit requested McCool's phone number did not return voice messages.)

Nancy noticed other signs. At home, Chris sometimes went outside to carry on phone conversations. He also had a second cell phone, which Nancy knew about but believed Chris was trying to hide from her. He had never done this before, and since she was a "smartened up" industry insider, she was sure that whatever he was concealing did not pertain to business. Of course, she had been taunting him about the decline of their sex life, and their relationship had taken on a full-throated slash-and-burn dynamic. Perhaps Chris was just taunting her back.

On June 17, Nancy returned home while Chris split the distance between Dothan and Fayetteville with a show in Columbus, Georgia. Whatever they talked about that day prompted Nancy's last recorded text message fulminations. At 4:01 p.m., she transmitted: *"Grow up!"* Twenty-two minutes later: *"Answer the phone I need to know what the plan is."* And at 4:35: *"If I end up having to throw away any food again for tonight and tomorrow I will not be cooking any meals for anyone for a very long time."*

Chris arrived home from Columbus at sixteen minutes past midnight on Monday, June 18. Letting himself in through the security gate, he apparently failed to deactivate the alarm. The Fayette County 911 Center was alerted and a sheriff's deputy was dispatched for what would be the first of two times in eight days. At 12:43 a.m., user code 17 was typed onto the security system keypad, disabling what in this case was a false alarm.

Later that day Nancy spoke on the phone for nearly two hours with her old friend Pam Clark in Tennessee. Clark was the widow of Brian Hildebrand, a wrestler and referee who had died of cancer. Nancy told Pam that Daniel was attending a summer horse-riding day camp at next-door neighbor Holly's. The women also discussed Nancy's concerns over the search for a school for him now that he had graduated from a preschool kindergarten program. But most of all, they talked about Nancy's ongoing struggles with Chris over money, sex, and control. Nancy specifically mentioned the arguments over the life insurance policy and her suspicions of an affair.

Financial security and sexual fidelity aside, Nancy described Chris's mood swings as becoming unbearable; he was at the point of picking a fight over almost nothing. She talked about needing to get away to visit her parents in Florida or her sister in North Carolina, or even move to Florida with Daniel.

Nancy also said Chris had been physically abusive, and she was afraid of him. She was keeping evidence of her husband's domestic violence in a safe place. She had a bad feeling.

"If anything happens to me," Nancy told Pam Clark,

"make sure people know that Chris did it."*

* * *

On Tuesday, June 19, Chris flew to Charlotte for a WWE TV taping. He returned to Georgia on Wednesday morning. The week proceeded as Chris's down time always did: catching up on sleep, visits to the tanning parlor and the gym. He talked to his friend James Robison, a manager at Partners II Pizza in Peachtree City, about plans for the Fourth of July. Since befriending Benoit years earlier at the gym, Robison had become the facilitator of a family tradition on Independence Day. He would secure a parking space for Chris next to the back entrance of the restaurant at Aberdeen Plaza near Lake Peachtree, then whisk Chris, Nancy, and Daniel upstairs to a reasonably private booth, from where they could look out the window and enjoy the waterfront fireworks without being bothered.

At 8:30 Friday morning, Chris dropped off Daniel at Holly's horse camp. Holly would tell Detective Harper that she found it strange that Chris pulled up and drove off so "quickly and recklessly." At least he drove Daniel to the door this time; the day before he had simply left the boy at the end of the driveway.

Chris drove on to Carrollton, forty miles northwest, for an appointment with his personal doctor, Phil

---

* In Nancy's safety deposit box at the Wachovia Bank branch in Peachtree City, sheriff's investigators found photos of Nancy with facial bruises. However, they determined that these documented the period of her earlier marriage to Kevin Sullivan. No photos were known to exist of the times Chris struck her.

Astin. The appointment wasn't until 12:30 p.m. Benoit may have stopped on the way for a bite to eat at one of favorite spots, Moe's Southwest Grill in Peachtree City. Benoit saw Astin every couple of months for routine check-ups and to replenish a raft of prescriptions. This time Chris said he had no special physical complaints — just the usual aches and pains — but added that he was mildly depressed and wanted to start taking Zoloft again. He discussed his marriage, saying Nancy had been acting "moody and bitchy" lately, and wondering if she was experiencing the onset of menopause. Not very likely at age forty-three, but "I agreed to see her professionally" after the Fourth of July "and agreed not to mention our conversation or his conversation to her," Astin would tell the sheriff in a written statement. Chris chatted with the office staff, as usual, and posed for a picture, and signed a few autographs for other patients in the waiting room.

On the drive home, Benoit talked on his cell with Hardcore Holly, who asked him how things were with Nancy. "She's been acting like Hitler, but we're working it out," Chris said. He met up with another wrestler friend, Ray Rawls, at the McDonald's off the I-85 Peachtree City/Tyrone exit. Like many younger wrestlers, Rawls — who worked under the name Rick Michaels — considered Benoit a model of professionalism. But Rawls had additional reasons for admiring him. A few years earlier, after working his way up from regional independent promotions, Rawls had gotten a shot with WWE. The company turned out not to be that interested in Rawls as a wrestler, but he was a talented tailor, and a number of the guys, Benoit among them, hired him to make their customized wrestling tights. Chris wore long tights, the kind that cover your legs, and he was a perfectionist about them, as he was with every aspect of his craft. He was like Michael Jordan with basketball shoes, discarding each pair after just a few matches. Over the course of just a couple of years, Benoit commissioned Rawls to make him around 120 pairs of tights, at several hundred dollars a pop.

And Chris was a generous tipper; when Rawls delivered the goods, he invariably got a check for at least $100 above the quoted price — even more if Chris forgot his checkbook and wound up paying later. That had happened a few months earlier, and the two made a plan to meet at Atlanta Hartsfield International Airport as Chris returned from a tour. Inadvertently, the incident gave Rawls a ringside seat for the disintegration of the Benoit marriage. Nancy, with Daniel in tow, showed up at the terminal to greet Chris, too, but when the plane landed, he wasn't on it. There was no explanatory phone message, and Nancy stormed off. The next day, Chris explained to Rawls that he'd overslept and missed his flight, which struck the latter as odd. Why hadn't Chris just called his wife and spared her the inconvenience of driving to the airport for nothing?

Yet another reason Rawls liked Chris had nothing to do with money. In 2005, WWE fired Rawls after he was arrested for sexual exploitation of a minor. Still, Chris kept up their connection. "I live in a glass house myself, so I don't throw stones," he said.

Rawls usually met Chris at the same McDonald's off the freeway. Often Daniel was tagging along and Rawls would give him a spare wrestler's mask or some other trinket. This time, because Chris was returning from Dr. Astin's, he was alone. Benoit handed Rawls a check for $650, and Rawls gave Chris two sets of tights, one for him and one to pass along to another wrestler, Chris Masters.

Rawls and Benoit talked shop. Ray wanted to know how Chris felt about having been moved recently from wwe's Raw roster to ecw, the company's least-watched brand. "As long as I can wrestle, that's all I care about," Chris replied.

When Rawls mentioned that he had been working hard and was tired, Benoit perked up. He said he knew the perfect pick-me-up: a mixture of Goody's Headache Powder, Red Bull energy drink, and "Yellow Jackets." The latter was an ephedra-based diet pill, banned several years earlier by the Food and Drug Administration, but generic knockoffs of indeterminate pharmacology continued to be sold over the counter at places like gas station convenience stores. (One drug expert explained this category of unregulated and easily obtained borderline products as a popular and low-cost pathway to a "hillbilly high.") No matter how tired he was, Chris said, the concoction "makes me feel like Superman."

"Chris insisted that I get some Goody's with Red Bull and Yellow Jackets right away," Rawls recalled. "There was a BP service station across the way, and he said BP carried Yellow Jackets. He told me to follow him there in my car. But they didn't have any. Then Chris said he was sure he'd find them at the BP closer to his house and he'd call me back when he did."

As Benoit sped off in his Hummer, Rawls thought, This guy is *wired*.

* * *

Back home, Chris talked on the phone to Kyle Burdg, a salesman at a local Hummer dealership, about selling one of their vehicles, and he ordered a call by Aqua Pro, the company that serviced the swimming pool. He talked to Chavo. He talked to Nancy, who was shopping at the local Publix supermarket for that evening's family cookout on the grill on the back deck. When the pool guys, Patrick Sterling and Andrew Webb, arrived, they saw Chris, flipping meat on the grill, and Daniel, both in swimming trunks.

That night, what Nancy had been fearing happened.

Records show that at 9:25 p.m., the 411 information number processed a request from the Benoit home phone for the number of the Fayetteville police. The number given out was an obsolete, non-emergency number, but in any case it wasn't called. Could Nancy not have known that, even though they had a Fayetteville postal address, they were located in an unincorporated area of the county and thus under the jurisdiction of the Fayette County Sheriff's Office, not the city of Fayetteville Police Department? (This awareness would have been underscored if she were awake at the time of the false alarm several nights earlier when Chris forgot to enter the shutoff pass code as he went through the gate. The responding agency that night was the county sheriff, not the city police.)

The possibility that an abortive effort to reach law enforcement might have been undertaken by Daniel, not Nancy, is tantalizing — and, if true, heartbreaking.

At 9:32, records show, there was a call from the Benoit home phone to next-door neighbor Holly's cell, then another a minute later, and another at 10 p.m., though no voice messages were left. Three days later, after she led the sheriff's deputies to the grisly scene on three different floors, Holly would recall the ringing of the phone on Friday night and wish she had answered. Maybe she could have done something.

* * *

At 8:30 Saturday morning, Chris left Holly a voice message: Was Daniel supposed to be at horse camp today? If so, he couldn't make it because he was sick.

When Holly picked up the message in the afternoon, she remarked to her husband that it was strange — Nancy, of course, knew the camp was on weekday mornings only. And with Chris's "somewhat antisocial" ways (as she would describe them to sheriff's investigators), it was uncharacteristic for him to initiate a conversation.

At 3:01 p.m., Holly called Chris back. They talked for nine minutes. Chris asked if anyone in her family had been sick. He said he was asking because Daniel had been up all night with food poisoning. Chris felt bad that he could do nothing for him. Nancy also had food poisoning, but just a touch, not as bad. Chris said he, personally, was fine, and Nancy and Daniel wanted to lay low for a few days and recover. Chris sounded very calm. Later Holly would realize that Chris had been discouraging her from calling or visiting Nancy, with whom she talked a lot.

* * *

A young wrestler named Michael Parker, who had just been released after a tryout with WWE, had left Chris a message on his cell, apparently about office politics. At 1:57 p.m., Chris left a return voice message, which Parker

75

would preserve and share with investigators. Many of Chris's words sounded slurred. He acknowledged, "I'm talking shit, I don't know what the details [of your situation] are off the top of my head." Chris said, "It sounds like you got shafted over and that really fuckin' sucks. . . . Nothing is better than experience and you've got that. . . . Hope you're doing well, I've missed you the last couple of weeks, wanted to point that out. When you can, give me a call."

∗ ∗ ∗

At 3:49 p.m. Saturday, Chris was on his desktop computer. He did a search for "Elija" on Google. One of the links there was information about the prophet Elijah on Wikipedia.com, and Chris went to that page at 4:02.

The New Testament's Book of Kings, Chapter 17, tells the story of Elijah being sent to a widow. The son of the widow dies and Elijah takes the child from his mother and stretches out on him three times in his own bed. Elijah pleads to God to restore the boy's soul to his body. "Yahweh listened to the voice of Elijah; and the soul of the child came into him again, and he revived. Eijah took the child, and brought him down out of the chamber into the house, and delivered him to his mother, and Elijah said, Behold, your son lives. The woman said to Elijah, Now I know that you are a man of God, and that the word of Yahweh in your mouth is truth."

Later the Benoit family pastor, George Dillard, would theorize that at that moment Chris might have been praying to God to return life to his family.

Another theory dovetails with Dillard's to surmise further that Daniel was not yet dead at that point, but Chris proceeded to kill him upon realizing that Nancy would not be revived and that the boy would be orphaned.

* * *

Chris continued talking to and texting with others through Saturday. On Sunday afternoon, not knowing that Benoit was dead, Chris Jericho texted, "Just heard that Wellington died of a heart attack this weekend." Shayne Bower ("Biff Wellington"), Benoit's old Stampede Wrestling stable mate, had been found dead in his bed at age forty-four.

Bower's best friend, Devon Fielding, told *SLAM! Wrestling*, "His dad said that the initial report was that they think he had a heart attack. . . . I know it wasn't drugs, because I know Shayne. He'd had a real battle with drugs, and he'd been clean for the last two years."

CHAPTER 6

Tribute to a Murderer

JUST AS THE EYES ARE THE WINDOWS to the soul, the decision by World Wrestling Entertainment to stage a three-hour tribute to Chris Benoit on the USA cable network's June 25, 2007, edition of *Raw* vividly illustrated the depravity at the heart of a peculiar genre. But tepid moralism exaggerates or misunderstands the lesson. Or to put it more precisely, the exaggeration becomes an excuse for the misunderstanding. While respectable opinion can legitimately lament the cliché of wrestling's festival of poor taste, the lament soon becomes its own cliché, and does nothing to prevent more performers from dying — by the bushel. An intelligent perspective on the Benoit tribute goes on to take a hard look at everything a huge corporation achieved when it brought its considerable resources to bear on containing the fallout of the Benoit crime.

Dan Abrams, on MSNBC, was among those who, at the time, denounced "spending three hours celebrating a guy . . . the authorities now say is a murderer." Worse, the tribute plotline echoed, mocked, and, in its inimitably weird way, validated the sentimental exploitation of previous non-homicidal wrestling deaths for TV ratings. The most pungent ironies began — but, like all wrestling "angles," never really ended — with the fact that this particular tribute happened to bump an already planned and fictitious parody show in which WWE chairman Vince McMahon's own violent death was to have been memorialized.

Still, the prosaic questions raised by the *Raw* tribute are much more troubling than the postmodernist mind games of a TV show cranked out on the fly. As critics speculated, but never followed through on, McMahon and his key people did indeed know that Benoit was the killer well before 8 p.m. eastern time on June 25. So, how much earlier did they know? Why did they want to know? And what did they plan to do about it? Those questions are the basis of the next chapters of this book. The answers are not clear-cut.

The next day, June 26, WWE would issue a press release headlined, "WWE Shares Internal Timeline and Details Relating to Chris Benoit Tragedy." A facsimile of the release is on the following two pages.

After closely examining WWE's asserted timeline of the Benoit death weekend, we can say that, unsurprisingly, it was sliced, diced, and ground through a processor of lawyers and PR specialists. But we can also say that the timeline is wildly implausible.

As this project unfolded, WWE lawyer Jerry McDevitt sent me a series of legal threats over some of the content of my blog. Tellingly, though, neither McDevitt nor anyone else from WWE has ever challenged the veracity of the conclusion that the Benoit *Raw* tribute was broadcast with substantial knowledge by the decision-makers that the Benoit family deaths were not a random triple

FOR IMMEDIATE RELEASE

WWE® Shares Internal Timeline And Details Relating To Chris Benoit Tragedy

STAMFORD, Conn., June 26, 2007 – World Wrestling Entertainment today released additional details of what it knows concerning communication with Chris Benoit and authorities before and after the tragic double homicide-suicide involving Benoit, his wife Nancy, and his son, Daniel.

WWE's timeline of events began on Saturday:

- On Saturday, June 23, Chris Benoit was slated to appear at a WWE live event in Beaumont, Texas. That afternoon, Benoit contacted WWE to inform them that his wife and child were ill, and that he would not be able to attend the show.

- WWE executives rebooked Benoit's flight for the following morning, allowing Benoit to miss the Beaumont event and making alternate arrangements for him to attend the pay-per-view event in Houston on Sunday.

- WWE employees attempted to confirm with Benoit his travel plans but were unable to contact him.

- Early Sunday morning, between 3:51 and 3:58 a.m., Benoit sent five text messages to co-workers:

  Text Message 1 to two co-workers (sent 6/24 at 3:53am)- Chris Benoit's cell phone
  "My physical address is 130 Green Meadow Lane, Fayetteville Georgia. 30215"

  Text Message 2 to two co-workers (sent 6/24 at 3:53am)- Chris Benoit's cell phone
  "The dogs are in the enclosed pool area. Garage side door is open"

  Text Message 3 to two co-workers (sent 6/24 at 3:54am)- Nancy Benoit's cell phone
  "My physical address is 130 Green Meadow Lane. Fayetteville Georgia. 30215"

  Text Message 4 to two co-workers (sent 6/24 at 3:55am)- Nancy Benoit's cell phone
  "My physical address is 130 Green Meadow Lane.

81

Fayetteville Georgia. 30215

Text Message 5 to one co-worker (sent 6/24 at 3:58am)- Nancy Benoit's cell phone
"My address is 130 Green Meadow Lane. Fayetteville Georgia. 30215"

- Throughout the day on Sunday, WWE made numerous attempts to contact Benoit both at home and at local hospitals in the Atlanta area. As of 11:00 p.m., WWE officials were unable to establish contact with Chris Benoit.

- At 12:30 p.m. on Monday, June 25, WWE officials were notified of the text messages sent to the co-workers the previous day. By 12:45 p.m., WWE had contacted Fayetteville County Sheriff's office requesting they check on the Benoit family.

- Fayetteville County Sheriffs office made contact with WWE at approximately 4:00 p.m. advising that they had entered the house of Chris Benoit and found three deceased bodies – an adult male, adult female and a male child. WWE was told that Benoit's home was now considered a major crime scene.

- The decision to cancel the live event scheduled in Corpus Christi that night was made between 4:00 and 5:00 p.m. In keeping with company policy, and with limited knowledge regarding facts of the case, WWE choose to air a memorial dedicated to the career of Chris Benoit. As facts emerged surrounding the case, all tributes to Chris Benoit were removed both on-air and on WWE.com.

WWE was stunned and saddened by the details released today by local authorities and is continuing to monitor the ongoing investigation.

-30-

Media Contact: Jennifer McIntosh, (818) 269-5621 - cell
Gary Davis, (203) 353-5066
Kevin Hennessy, (203) 352-8657

murder, but a double murder-suicide committed by Chris. That finding is unassailably true.

* * *

At 3 p.m. eastern time on June 25, Detectives Ethon Harper and Joshua Shelton joined Deputy Mundy and Lieutenant Alden, along with next-door neighbor Holly, at the crime scene. Lieutenant Tommy Pope (later promoted to captain) arrived minutes later. Pope supervised the ongoing tasks of assembling evidence and preserving its chain of custody. Harper did his own quick inspection, confirming the obvious signs that Chris had murdered Nancy and Daniel before hanging himself. Harper then drove eight miles back into central Fayetteville, to the Fayette County Justice Center, where he obtained a search warrant from Circuit Judge Christopher Edwards. Harper called Pope to advise him that a signed warrant was in hand before making the eighteen-minute return trip to Green Meadow Lane.

The head of the Crime Scene Unit team, Lieutenant Tray Powell, oversaw the photographs and, with Bee Huddleston of the coroner's office, arranged for the removal of the three bodies to the Georgia Bureau of Investigation Crime Lab. The task of notifying family members fell to Detective Bo Turner.

A minor controversy would ensue over the failure to collect blood tissue samples from the bodies at the scene. Powell observed a discolored smudge on Chris's left index finger near the knuckle on the thumb side, and hypothesized that it was a friction burn from tying the knots of the cable that bound Nancy. Powell also saw dried blood on the bridge of Chris's nose and in the nail bed of his right index finger. The lieutenant decided to transport the bodies to the crime lab "as is" and to have tissue samples collected during the autopsy. At the lab the next day, however, Powell could no longer locate the areas of suspected blood, and he was therefore unable to collect samples. Powell would write in his report, "The blood that was noted on his nose . . . had been removed by the moisture of the body or rubbed off in the bag. The blood splatter noted on his left index finger showed no signs of injury either. I noted no marking of injury where the blood smear was on his nose. The blood was . . . most likely produced by another source. The source likely being the wife, Nancy Benoit."

Searching for motives, Detective Harper collected paperwork, most of which was in folders in Nancy's office above the garage: financial records, household utility and credit card statements, insurance and tax documents, medical reports, business and legal correspondence, fan mail.

Inside a small refrigerator in the office's wet bar, Detective Mitchell Howard found several small bottles labeled "Recombinant Human Growth Hormone" from a Chinese company called GeneScience Pharmaceutical Co. Ltd. The bag with the growth hormone bottles also contained three insulin syringes.

A Hewlett Packard desktop computer was removed from the office for a forensic examination. Later the Benoit side of the family would dispute the thoroughness of that exam, which involved making an image of the hard drive with a tool called FTK and creating an index of the data files.*

---

* The sheriff did not release the full Internet and email history, images, and

The cell phones near Chris's body and the home phone answering machine were impounded. Before removing the answering machine, Detectives Shelton and Howard played back and made a secondary digital audio recording of the messages on it. The recording, ultimately released with the public records, was crude due to background noise during the general commotion at the crime scene.

In the upstairs master bedroom, Lieutenant Powell and Detective Bryan Hergesell spotted two boxes with prescription labels from Jones Pharmacy in Fayetteville. The prescribing physician was Phil Astin of Carrollton. The boxes contained March and May 2007 prescriptions of testosterone 200 mg/ml. That night and the next day, investigators would locate supplies of many other prescription medications for both Chris and Nancy. These included Carisoprodol (Soma), a muscle relaxer; Lorcet (Hydrocodone), a narcotic pain reliever; Alprazolam (Xanax), which is used to treat anxiety and panic disorders; Naproxen, an anti-inflammatory drug; Ambien, a sedative or sleeping drug; and Sertraline (Zoloft) and Cymbalta, both antidepressants. Still later, over a period of weeks, Nancy Benoit's family members staying at the house would discover additional steroids, syringes, and other prescription and over-the-counter drugs in a suitcase and in a walk-in closet.

---

video files, asserting that they were exempt under Georgia open records law: "None of this information is relevant to the incident and had any bearing on the investigation." Whether the entirety of the computer's Internet and email history was irrelevant seems highly questionable, but at least the assertion of a legal exemption was made directly. As will be seen later, the sheriff in other areas fudged the very existence of a supporting record.

* * *

At around 3:30 p.m. mountain time (5:30 eastern) on June 25, Margaret Benoit, Chris's mother, answered the phone at the home she and her husband shared near Sherwood Park, a suburb of Edmonton, Alberta. The caller was Carl DeMarco, who had risen through the ranks as the person who drove former champion Bret Hart to his appearances in Canada. DeMarco was then the president of WWE Canada.

"I considered Chris one of my best friends . . ." DeMarco began.

Confused, Margaret Benoit said, "Why are you telling me this?"

Only then did DeMarco realize that the Benoits hadn't yet gotten the news. He made an excuse and told Margaret he would call her right back.

In Georgia, Detective Turner hadn't called either the Benoit family in Alberta or the Toffolonis, Nancy's side, in Florida.* Perhaps the Georgia authorities were hoping to assemble more information before talking to the

---

* The publicly released home answering machine messages would include a series of late Monday afternoon/early Monday evening calls from Nancy's parents, Paul and Maureen Toffoloni, escalating in confusion and worry. Though neither DeMarco nor Turner would grant an interview to confirm this, it seems overwhelmingly likely that DeMarco called Turner or got a message to him after DeMarco spoke the first time with Margaret Benoit. Also on the answering machine was a message left at some undetermined point by Daniel Benoit for his father, whom the little boy affectionately called "pooh-bear." Finally, the answering machine still retained — probably for sentimental reasons — the very last known recordings of the voice of Eddie Guerrero, in two messages left the day before Guerrero died in Minneapolis in 2005. The answering machine audio is included in the companion disk. See "Order the DVD" at the back of this book.

families. But some time before 4:30 p.m. mountain time (6:30 eastern), Turner did call Margaret Benoit. As promised, DeMarco then also called Margaret back.

DeMarco — whose concern the family would describe as genuine and appreciated — took note of how distraught Margaret became. DeMarco called the Royal Canadian Mounted Police detachment in Strathcona County and requested that Emergency Medical Services attend to Mrs. Benoit.

At 4:47 mountain time, RCMP Constable Rob Morris drove to Sherwood Park to assist the medical team. While en route, Morris would write in his report, "The following information was confirmed: The son who had passed away was World Wrestling Entertainment star Chris Benoit, along with his wife, Nancy, and their 7 year old son, Daniel. Information was received of this by Detective TURNER of Atlanta/Fayetteville Police [*sic*] and the president of World Wrestling Entertainment Canada, Carl DEMARCO. Det. TURNER had already notified Margaret of the incident."

Five minutes later Morris called Turner to confirm details:

> Detective Turner had already spoken with Chris's mother, Margaret BENOIT, and informed her of Chris's passing. The incident was being investigated as an alleged murder-suicide. . . .*

---

* Facsimiles of the RCMP "Occurrence summary" and "General Occurrence Report" are included in the companion disk. See "Order the DVD" at the back of this book.

Morris also called DeMarco, who said he had enlisted Scott Zerr, an Edmonton journalist who was close to Chris Benoit, to drive to the house and lend his additional support to Margaret and Michael Benoit. Margaret had called Mike at work and asked him to come home immediately, without telling him why. When Mike pulled into the driveway around 4:45, Zerr greeted him outside "and told me that Chris had taken the lives of Nancy and Daniel and then taken his own life," Mike would later write in an email to me. "This information had been given to him that afternoon by wwe."*

Forty minutes earlier in California, wrestling journalist Dave Meltzer had received the same news in a call from Canada. Meltzer said the call came from one of Chris Benoit's best friends, whom a wwe executive had told matter-of-factly of the murder-suicide at around 5:30 eastern time. Meltzer would later confirm to me that the wwe executive was DeMarco.

According to wwe's published timeline, "In keeping with company policy, and with limited knowledge

---

* After some of the information in this chapter was published on my blog, Zerr denied to Josh Stewart, a wrestling columnist for the *Long Island Press*, that he was the one who had told Mike Benoit that Chris was the perpetrator. Mike linked Zerr's puzzling denial to Mike's earlier refusal to sign a legal release authorizing a book Zerr was planning to write. Mike reemphasized the accuracy of my account and said he believed Zerr to be part of "a coordinated attempt to discredit" my work.

Zerr — whom I have never met or spoken to — also falsely told others that an essay I had published months after the Benoit deaths failed to mention Chris's concussion syndrome, and he spoke of me in disparaging terms to Mike Benoit. A wrestling insider told me, "The fact that Zerr would run you down in combination with the denial shows it's likely coming directly from DeMarco, and that they have no defense. DeMarco is the type — clumsy in covering his tracks."

regarding facts of the case, WWE chose to air a memorial dedicated to the career of Chris Benoit," making this decision between 4 p.m. and 5 p.m. eastern.

* * *

World Wrestling Entertainment had substantial experience in public relations crisis management, specifically in inconvenient high-profile deaths. In 1997, Brian Pillman was found dead in a motel room in Bloomington, Minnesota, outside Minneapolis, just as he was supposed to have a leading role in a pay-per-view that was about to be broadcast from the Kiel Center in St. Louis. McMahon shot a straightforward opening cut-in, explaining to the audience why Pillman wasn't there, and carried on with the show. The next night *Raw* was devoted to a Pillman tribute; McMahon even had Pillman's tearful widow on a satellite hookup discussing his lost battle with various addictions.

In 1999, another pay-per-view was just getting under way in Kansas City when wrestler Owen Hart crashed into the ring from the rafters of Kemper Arena. In a stunt entrance gone awry, Hart's harness broke and he was killed on impact. Again, McMahon continued with the show — later maintaining, in part, that he feared a riot by fans if the show were canceled — and he dedicated the next night's *Raw* to a tribute to Hart.

In 2005 Eddie Guerrero also got the full tearjerker treatment on *Raw*. In the age of reality TV, the Guerrero tribute garnered great ratings. And the Owen Hart tribute had been one of the two most-watched episodes in *Raw* history.

By coincidence, exactly two weeks before the Benoit

tribute — on June 11, 2007 — McMahon had pulled off a modern-day poor man's version of Orson Welles' *War of the Worlds* hoax. That night's *Raw*, from the Wachovia Arena in Wilkes-Barre, Pennsylvania, revolved around a "Mr. McMahon Appreciation Night," which turned into an orgy of tragedy and terror at the conclusion, when a bomb exploded inside McMahon's limousine just as he was entering it. The explosion had been shot over the course of the previous two nights, then edited into the live Monday night feed, in a stunt production coordinated by Zenith Pyrotechnology of Deer Park, New York, which secured local permits and had the area blocked off.

WWE's corporate website, designed to separate public disclosures to investors from wrestling story lines, merged the two in a news release whose tongue-in-cheek nature sailed over the heads of some fans:

> The shocking ending raised a myriad of questions: Could Mr. McMahon have survived the fiery explosion? And who could've committed such a heinous act? Although full details have not been disclosed, initial reports indicate that Mr. McMahon is presumed dead. An official investigation into Monday night's events is currently underway with no one being ruled out as a suspect. Throughout the night, people from Mr. McMahon's past — from Donald Trump to Snoop Dogg to Bob Costas to Stone Cold Steve Austin — had less than flattering things to say about the WWE Chairman, but would any go so far as to actually blow him up? The question of "whodunit," as well as the fate of Mr. McMahon, will be on everyone's minds as the WWE saga continues on "Monday Night RAW" on USA (9 p.m. ET/8C).

On the CNBC business news network, sports business specialist Darren Rovell questioned whether the fake death broke any laws, and concluded that the answer was no: "McMahon isn't creating any sort of phony documentation or cashing in on a life insurance policy; it doesn't seem like there's any exposure here. *But I still think there's a possibility the organization could be sued by a shareholder.* By announcing that he is 'presumed dead' on their official website, they could be charged with misleading stockholders."

WWE responded to Rovell's report by releasing a deadpan statement adding him to the list of suspects in McMahon's murder.*

On the June 18 edition of *Raw*, Stephanie McMahon Levesque — Vince's daughter and a WWE executive, as well as an on-screen WWE personality and the wife of wrestler Paul Levesque ("Hunter Hearst Helmsley" or "Triple H") — confirmed that her father was "presumed dead" and said the next week's show would be a celebration of his snuffed-out life.

Instead, in mid-afternoon in Corpus Christi, Vince

---

* Generally speaking, does WWE, a publicly traded company listed on the New York Stock Exchange, run afoul of federal securities law prohibitions against issuing materially false statements when it hypes wrestling story lines on its corporate website, outside the boundaries of its entertainment television shows, website, and magazines? In a related example, WWE in the spring of 2008 staged a news conference to announce that boxer Floyd Mayweather was being paid $20 million to appear at *WrestleMania* — a figure surely many multiples higher than Mayweather's actual payoff. If there were factual misstatements in WWE's published internal timeline for Benoit, the same issue might arise. And in June 2009, WWE shares plunged seven percent after a TV storyline, supported by a USA cable news release, had Donald Trump purchasing WWE's Raw brand.

gathered the talent ringside at Citizen Bank Center in Corpus Christi and informed them that the Benoits had been found dead. McMahon did not elaborate. The wrestlers were in street clothes — some in the black suits they had been asked to bring for "Mr. McMahon's" goof memorial. Chris Masters saw Randy Orton, a star wrestler, break into tears talking with Michael Hayes, the head writer and a former wrestler. Masters later told WrestleZone.com that there had been "a buzz about some odd text messages Chris had sent to Chavo Guerrero and one of the ECW referees." Masters suspected the worst. "I mean, how many different scenarios can there be? Either home invasion or Chris snapping. Not many others shared my thoughts on a double murder-suicide."

McMahon told the crew that, in lieu of wrestling, Benoit's colleagues would give interview testimonials and remembrances on *Raw*. McMahon said anyone who wanted to go home had permission to do so. Few, if any, took up the offer — there was comfort in remaining enveloped in the numbers of this spontaneous wake. Ted DiBiase, a retired wrestler who had become an evangelical Christian minister, had been flown to Texas to be part of the McMahon death story line; now DiBiase found himself enlisted as a real-life grief counselor.

At 8 p.m. eastern time on June 25, Vince McMahon stood in center ring in the empty arena. Eyes blurred by tears, voice choking and reduced to the hoarse growl characteristic for him at the end of a long day of stress, McMahon broke character as he delivered the *Raw* opening:

Tonight's story line was to have been the alleged demise of my character, Mr. McMahon. However, in reality, WWE superstar Chris Benoit, his wife Nancy and their son Daniel are dead. Their bodies were discovered this afternoon in their new suburban Atlanta home. The authorities are undergoing an investigation. We here in the WWE can only offer our condolences to the extended family of Chris Benoit. And the only other thing we can do at this moment is, tonight, pay tribute to Chris Benoit. We will offer you some of the most memorable moments in Chris's professional life and you will hear, tonight, comments from his peers — those here, his fellow performers — those here, who loved Chris and admired him so much. So tonight will be a three-hour tribute to one of the greatest WWE superstars of all time. Tonight we pay tribute to Chris Benoit.

With that, taped highlights of Benoit's career were played to the accompaniment of the song "One Thing" by the Canadian grunge band Finger Eleven. *Raw* announcers Jim Ross and Jerry "The King" Lawler reflected on Benoit's legacy. Retired wrestling legend "Stone Cold" Steve Austin spoke via videotape. John Bradshaw Layfield talked about Benoit's devotion to his family. Tazz, C.M. Punk, Dean Malenko, Triple H and his wife Stephanie, and others said their pieces. The tribute culminated with footage of Benoit's 2004 *WrestleMania* championship victory, followed by the emotional in-ring celebration with Nancy, Daniel, and Eddie Guerrero.

One of the live testimonials was by William Regal, one of Benoit's original Fayette County wrestling neighbors. Regal's segment came off as unintentionally chilling. Just before Regal went out for the shoot, Layfield remarked to him, "You don't think Chris killed that boy, do you?" Spooked, Regal proceeded to deliver an eerily detached eulogy; while calling Chris the best wrestler he had ever faced, Regal also said he would rather reserve comment on anything else until the facts came in.

"If you watch the *Raw* tribute carefully, it doesn't appear that the wrestlers, as a group, had an inkling that it was murder-suicide," Meltzer said. "But the McMahon family had to know." Meltzer's assessment was too generous. Though the power of denial cannot be discounted, my investigation has unearthed plenty of evidence that a substantial group of people had "an inkling."

During the hour from 10 p.m. to 11 p.m. (eastern time) — two thirds of the way through the tribute's live feed — Doug Evans of Fox 5 News in Atlanta became the first journalist to report to a wide audience that the Fayette County crime scene investigation was focusing on murder-suicide. Minutes later the WWE website's own home page was headlined, "Double Murder-Suicide," with the text: "It has been ruled that the deaths . . . were the result of a double murder-suicide from within the home. WWE.com will have more as soon as it becomes available."

"Here is what has always bothered me," Evans said in a later email to me. "I got a tip about the murder not long after the investigators arrived, and it came from inside the gates. Pretty fresh you would think, right? I started heading immediately to Fayette County. On my way, a radio reporter from Canada called me (he was given my cell number by our staff in Atlanta) and he wanted to know about the murders and suicide. He said it was already on the WWE web page. How did that happen so fast? My source couldn't reveal the names at the time but gave me the location. However, there it was already in full detail for the whole world to read. How did that happen?"

The last hour of the Benoit tribute forged ahead on USA cable, after which the repeat feed to the West Coast was broadcast intact. The WWE website home page, alongside the news bulletin, continued to stream a tribute video package along with exclusive studio-produced testimonials.

Inside the ring and in TV skits, WWE's verbal agility is always striking, and it was on full display here. The company had concealed the overwhelming suspicion of murder-suicide, of which at least higher-ups had been aware since, at the latest, around the hour of four to five o'clock eastern time. Turning on a dime, WWE.com now exaggerated the report of the preponderant investigative theory, calling it a "ruling." At the same time, the phrase "within the home" continued to keep the identity of the killer vague. Recalling the murder of comic actor Phil Hartman by his wife, many of Chris's fans continued to hold out the perverse hope that Nancy, and not Chris, would prove to be the perpetrator.

Of course, that was not to be. The next night, at the start of another cable show, on the Sci Fi network, McMahon said Chris Benoit would never be mentioned again on WWE television. By then all references to Benoit had been expunged from the website, and all Benoit-related videos and merchandise were being pulled from physical and virtual store shelves "as facts emerged surrounding the case," according to the company's timeline. The passive construction "as facts emerged" was key. When they emerged to Vince McMahon did not compute; only when they emerged to the public at a pace and in a manner McMahon tightly controlled.

It was the end of the following week, Friday, July 6, by the time McMahon got around to calling Mike Benoit in Alberta. "I suppose that I could have called earlier," McMahon said. "But we were both trying to deal with this."

Screening calls, Benoit heard the message live as it came through on his answering machine. He chose not to pick up. Nor would he ever return McMahon's call.

CHAPTER 7

Chavo Guerrero, Scott Armstrong, the Text Messages, and the Two Timelines

HUNDREDS OF PRO WRESTLERS DIED young in the twenty or so years before the Chris Benoit tragedy. Some, like Brian Pillman and Eddie Guerrero, had heart disease brought on or exacerbated by abuse of steroids and other drugs. Some overdosed more overtly on recreational drugs like cocaine. Some committed suicide. Some suffered liver or kidney malfunction, which — like the forms of cancer sometimes associated with them — stemmed from alcohol and/or high doses of their pharmaceuticals of choice. Others met their ends in car crashes, in which fatigue or impairment played a part, and at least one was killed in a barroom brawl. Most rarely, but occasionally, others died in accidents inside the ring, like Owen Hart.

Prior to June 2007, however, no wrestler had ever murdered loved ones in a rampage so sensational that it made the cover of *People* magazine, fueled tabloid coverage, and for weeks commanded panel-discussion analysis and commentary on cable news networks. Principally for that reason, it is hard to pass judgment on Chavo Guerrero and Scott Armstrong if they initially weren't sure what to make of Chris Benoit's final text messages on Sunday, June 24. The Benoit murder-suicide was an event of unprecedented perplexity and ugliness. Guerrero and Armstrong couldn't fight the last war because there hadn't *been* a last war.

The two wrestler friends must have found further disorienting the sense that Benoit seemed poorly cast for the role of someone "going postal." By wrestling standards he was a straight arrow. He was also private and reserved outside the ring, and even if under stress in his marriage — an element worsened by the travel and image demands of his profession — he gave every indication of loving his wife and their child. Chris especially doted on Daniel.

So the first possibilities to occur to Guerrero and Armstrong naturally wouldn't have been successive garroting, neck-snapping, and hanging. To the extent they realized Chris was in serious trouble, their instinct would have been to protect him and protect their business. Expecting them to comprehend immediately the depth of that trouble may be unfair.

Still, informed speculation as to how and why Guerrero and Armstrong acted as they did cannot let them entirely off the hook. Even if they didn't grasp the picture on Saturday evening, Sunday morning, or Sunday afternoon, the full alarm was surely sounded by the time Benoit no-showed the Houston pay-per-view on Sunday night. At that point, it made no sense for friends and colleagues (or for WWE's well-staffed talent relations and security departments, reporting to company executives) to continue to scratch their heads in isolation instead of huddling and taking action. Specifically, it is not credible that Guerrero and Armstrong told no one (not just no "WWE officials," in the words of the company's timeline, however those are defined) about the text messages all day and night Sunday — if, indeed, that is what they maintain. To the public, they would have nothing to say (with one key exception, which we will get to). And law enforcement authorities either didn't ask them to say anything or censored the answers in the report on their investigation.

As for the company's assertion that "WWE officials" were unaware of the messages until 12:30 p.m. Monday — more than thirty hours after Benoit transmitted them, and an hour and a half after the company's security consultant made the last call to the Benoit home attempting to reach him — the chance is extremely slim that the left hand didn't know what the right hand was doing. This was sixteen hours after the curtain went up on the *Vengeance* pay-per-view, with a lineup of matches and story lines altered due to Benoit's absence. Confusion falls into place as a global explanation only if WWE deployed a chain of communications designed to give "plausible deniability" to Vince McMahon and his top aides.

And for the boss to have been so detached from the details of his wrestling intelligence and corporate decision-making would have been dramatically unlike him: McMahon was as involved an owner as you will find in any industry anywhere. Vince and his daughter Stephanie and son Shane and, even occasionally, wife-CEO Linda were themselves cast members of the WWE TV soap opera subplots. In his sixties, Vince still stepped between the ropes for a gimmick match a couple of times a year. In a 2001 *Playboy* magazine interview, McMahon discussed his hands-on management style. If someone was needed to help the stagehands pull cable for a camera operator at a TV shoot, he said, "I'll pull cable."

Guerrero and Armstrong's shared private explanation of the thirty-hour gap between the sending of Benoit's red-flag text messages and their acting on them is almost laughable — not only on its face but also because it contradicts that single public utterance on the subject by Guerrero.

Probing the meaning of WWE's timelines, with their interchangeable elements, is the subject of this chapter. The full and accurate story remains hazy, and the most responsible outcome is not to jump to a specific, Monday-morning-quarterback conclusion. The missing pieces, however, do concentrate the mind on wrestling's corporate culture of control and calculated ambiguity. Guerrero and Armstrong could have been playing fast and loose with the truth out of mere habit, because that's what wrestling and wrestlers do. Or they could have acted out of discomfort with the sudden attention focused on them in a scenario whose outcome they sincerely, if guiltily, determined they'd had no power to change. They could have believed that time-honored methods of working the marks would make that attention go away. And if that was their goal, they were largely vindicated by the general public's lack of stamina for getting to the bottom of the story.

Or they could have done what they did because they were so advised — or ordered. In the best of times, the wrestling business was never a secure place for talent; today a single company, WWE, and a single promoter, McMahon, call pretty much all the shots for just a few dozen top spots.

* * *

The text message angle of the investigation starts with the official and permanently published WWE timeline, reproduced on pages 81–82. This timeline was issued as a news release, dated June 26, and at the time of this book's publication, was still viewable at the corporate website at http://corporate.WWE.com/news/2007/2007_06_26_2.jsp.

But in addition, there was an earlier timeline, the text of which is reproduced on the following two pages.

This was first published on the WWE entertainment website on Tuesday night, June 26, but later pulled. Read one way, the two timelines complement each other. Read another way, the earlier and better-substantiated timeline contradicts the later and more circumspect one in subtle and disturbing ways. The latter seems intended to stand as WWE's final and authoritative words on the subject. It may have been spurred by Wall Street observers who criticized WWE's initial response for saying too much too soon — causing the company to revise, clarify, and come across as unhelpfully defensive and combative.*

The earlier and fuller version of the timeline illuminates the thirty-hour gap between text messages sent and bodies recovered. Even more significantly, it jibes with the consensus account — in the phone call logs and interviews of the Fayette County sheriff's report, as well

---

* On my blog, I originally called the earlier version "the Daily News timeline" because it was picked up most prominently on the *New York Daily News* website. Subsequent research on fan discussion boards, however, established that the timeline originated at http://www.WWE.com/inside/news/detailed benoittimeline before the company deleted it. After expunging the timeline, WWE also disowned it. In response to an email about this on September 25, 2008, Jennifer McIntosh, WWE's head of publicity, immediately wrote back:

Chris Benoit Timeline

A look at the final days of Chris Benoit's life:

Saturday, June 23, 2007

Chris Benoit was scheduled to appear at the WWE SmackDown live event in Beaumont, Texas.

3:30 p.m.
A co-worker received a voice message from Benoit. The message from Benoit stated he missed his flight and over slept and would be late to the WWE Live Event. The co-worker called Benoit back, Benoit confirmed everything he said in his voice message and sounded tired and groggy. Benoit then stated, "I love you". The co-worker stated that it was "out of context."

3:42 p.m.
The same co-worker was concerned with Benoit's tone and demeanor and called Benoit for a second time. Benoit did not answer the call and the co-worker left a message stating "just call me back."

3:44 p.m.
Benoit called the co-worker back stating he didn't answer the call because he was on the phone with Delta changing his flight. Benoit stated he had a real stressful day due to Nancy and Daniel being sick with food poisoning. They discussed travel plans for the WWE Tour of Texas with Benoit still sounding groggy at this point according to the co-worker.

4:30 p.m.
A co-worker who consistently travels with Benoit, called Benoit from outside Houston airport and Benoit answered. Benoit told the co-worker that Nancy was throwing up blood and that Daniel was also throwing up. Benoit thought they had food poisoning. Benoit stated he changed his flight and he would be arriving into Houston at 6:30 p.m. Benoit told the co-worker to drive onto the WWE event.

5:35 p.m.
Benoit called WWE Talent Relations stating that his son was throwing up and that he and Nancy were in the hospital with their son, and that Benoit would be taking a later flight into Houston, landing late, but would make the WWE live event in Beaumont.

6:10 p.m.
A representative of Talent Relations called Benoit. The representative from Talent Relations asked Benoit what time Benoit was getting into Beaumont. Benoit responded he was leaving Atlanta at 9:20 p.m. eastern time arriving into Houston at 9:24 p.m. central time. The representative from Talent Relations advised Benoit that it would be too late to make the WWE live event in Beaumont. Benoit apologized citing he had a family emergency. The representative from Talent Relations suggested to Benoit that instead of going to the WWE live event in Beaumont, Benoit should take the flight to Houston, rest up and be ready for the Vengeance Pay-Per-View event.

6:13 p.m.
The representative from Talent Relations called Benoit to reconfirm the travel plans with no answer from Benoit. The representative from Talent Relations left a voice message to take the flight and rest up.

Sunday, June 24, 2007

Text messages sent to co-workers from Chris Benoit and Nancy Benoit's cell phones:

Text Message 1
Sent to: Two co-workers (the same who had verbal correspondence with Benoit the day before)
From: Benoit's cell phone
When: 6/24 at 3:53 a.m.
Message: C, S. My physical address is 130 Green Meadow Lane. Fayetteville Georgia. 30215

Text Message 2
Sent to: Two co-workers (the same who had verbal correspondence with Benoit the day before)
From: Benoit's cell phone
When: 6/24 at 3:53 a.m.
Message: The dogs are in the enclosed pool area. Garage side door is open

Text Message 3
Sent to: Two co-workers (the same who had verbal correspondence with Benoit the day before)
From: Nancy Benoit's cell phone
When: 6/24 at 3:54 a.m.
Message: C, S. My physical address is 130 Green Meadow Lane. Fayetteville Georgia. 30215

Text Message 4
Sent to: Two Co-Workers (the same who had verbal correspondence with Benoit the day before)
From: Nancy Benoit's cell phone
When: 6/24 at 3:55 a.m.
Message: C, S. My physical address is 130 Green Meadow Lane. Fayetteville Georgia. 30215

Text Message 5
Sent to: A co-worker who consistently traveled with Benoit
From: Nancy Benoit's cell phone
When: 6/24 at 3:58am
Message: My address is 130 Green Meadow Lane. Fayetteville Georgia. 30215

WWE made several attempts to contact Benoit via phone and text messages, as well as, the local hospitals in the Atlanta area.

As of 11:00 p.m. Sunday night there was no contact made with Benoit.

Monday, June 25, 2007

12:30 p.m.
WWE was notified of text messages sent to the two co-workers.

12:45 p.m.
WWE contacted the Fayette County Sheriff's office and requested them to go to Benoit's residence.

4:00 p.m.
WWE received a call from the Fayette County Sheriff's office, advising that they entered the house of Benoit and found 3 deceased bodies (a male, a female and a child). The Fayette County Sheriff's office has secured the house as a "major crime scene" and that the Fayette County Sheriff's Office had no further information.

Source: From WWE.com

as from other sources — of Benoit's Saturday conversations with Guerrero, Armstrong, and others.

∗ ∗ ∗

The most devastating of those interactions was Benoit's
dialogue with Chavo Guerrero on Saturday afternoon, as
Chris agonized over still being in Georgia even though
he was scheduled to wrestle that night at the WWE show
in Beaumont, Texas.

According to the first version of the timeline, at
3:30 p.m., "A co-worker received a voice message from
Benoit. The message from Benoit stated he missed his
flight and overslept and would be late to the WWE Live
Event. The co-worker called Benoit back, Benoit confirmed everything he said in his voice message and
sounded tired and groggy. Benoit then stated, 'I love
you.'" (The timeline times are probably all intended to be
eastern time, but a possible one-hour discrepancy
between eastern and central time would not affect the
thrust of this part of the narrative.)

Reflecting on that conversation, the co-worker was
so unsettled by what sounded like an over-the-top
expression of affection, and by Benoit's overall "tone
and demeanor," that he called Benoit back twelve minutes later, leaving the message, "Just call me." Benoit

---

"Irv, Thanks for getting in touch with me. Can I get back to you on this
tomorrow? I'm traveling today and need to double check my files to make
sure I'm sending you the correct info. If you need it today, I'll ask my co-
worker Gary Davis [WWE vice president of corporate communications] to
help. Thanks, Jenny." McIntosh, however, did not get back to me the next day
or ever, and she did not return follow-up email and voice messages.

returned the call, though he didn't speak to the co-worker. In his message, Benoit managed to allay any urgent concerns by explaining that he was just having "a real stressful day due to Nancy and Daniel being sick with food poisoning," the co-worker recalled for the timeline.

That co-worker was Chavo Guerrero. In his Monday tribute interview on the WWE website, Guerrero would tell an Internet audience that Chris Benoit ended their last conversation by saying, "I love you" (though Guerrero added nothing in that online testimonial about how the line had struck him as odd).

Mike Benoit, Chris's father, told me Guerrero recounted the identical story to him. "Wrestlers conclude conversations by saying 'love you' or 'love ya, man' to each other all the time," Mike said, "but Chavo said he thought the way Chris said it that time was strange and out of context, so strange that Chavo decided to call back. Chavo left a message for Chris: 'Just let me know that you're OK.'"

The sheriff's report had more of the same:

> Guerrero advised Chris Benoit left him a message . . . saying he overslept and missed his flight. . . . Guerrero commented that Benoit sounded a little strange or depressed while they spoke [later]. Guerrero advised that after hanging up he called Benoit right back and asked him if he was ok. . . . Benoit stated he was just upset and tired due to Nancy and Daniel being sick with food poisoning.

At 4:30 p.m. Saturday, according to the early version of the timeline, another co-worker, "who consistently travels with Benoit, called Benoit from outside Houston airport and Benoit answered. Benoit told the co-worker that Nancy was throwing up blood and that Daniel was also throwing up. Benoit thought they had food poisoning. Benoit stated he changed his flight and he would be arriving into Houston at 6:30 p.m." Benoit told the colleague to drive on to the Beaumont event alone.

That second co-worker was Scott Armstrong, who told sheriff's investigators that he and Benoit "spoke about rental car and hotel room arrangements" and "Chris told him that Nancy and Daniel were sick and he may be late for the next show, but he would be there."

* * *

Benoit's travel plan, for either Saturday evening or Sunday morning, is a central mystery. This is where the earlier wwe.com timeline and the final corporate timeline stop overlapping and start clashing, suggesting why the company might have decided it was prudent to become less specific, if not downright misleading. Further, the known existing evidence fully supports the earlier version while casting deep shadows over the final one.

At 5:35, according to the first timeline, "Benoit called WWE Talent Relations stating that his son was throwing up and that he and Nancy were in the hospital with their son, and that Benoit would be taking a later flight into Houston, landing late, but would make the WWE live event in Beaumont." Thirty-five minutes later, "A representative of Talent Relations called Benoit" and asked "what time Benoit was getting into Beaumont." (After flying into Houston's George Bush Intercontinental Airport, he would need to rent a car and drive more than 100 miles in order to make the

Beaumont show.) Benoit said he would depart from
Atlanta at 9:20 eastern time and land in Houston more
than an hour later, at 9:24 central time. "The representative from Talent Relations advised Benoit that it
would be too late to make the WWE live event in
Beaumont. Benoit apologized, citing a family emergency. The representative from Talent Relations
suggested to Benoit that instead of going to the WWE
live event in Beaumont, Benoit should take the flight to
Houston, rest up and be ready for the Vengeance pay-
per-view event [in Houston on Sunday night]."

At 6:13 the WWE person "called Benoit to reconfirm
the travel plans with no answer from Benoit. The representative from Talent Relations left a voice message to
take the flight and rest up."

WWE's vice president of talent relations was John
Laurinaitis, a retired wrestler under the name "Johnny
Ace" and the brother of a more famous retired wrestler,
Joe Laurinaitis ("Road Warrior Animal"). The phone logs
confirm calls to Benoit's cell phone from the WWE office
in Stamford, Connecticut, on Saturday. (There would be
additional calls from the WWE office — including several
from John Laurinaitis's direct line — the next day.)

The final version of the WWE timeline on the corporate website includes two bullet points on Benoit's
Atlanta-to-Houston travel plans. They convey a somewhat different resolution on Saturday night:

> • WWE executives rebooked flight *for the following morning,*
> allowing Benoit to miss the Beaumont event and making
> alternate arrangements for him to attend the pay-per-view
> event in Houston on Sunday. *[Emphasis added.]*

- WWE employees attempted to confirm with Benoit his travel plans but were unable to contact him.

The distinction between a later Saturday evening flight and a Sunday morning flight is trivial in the sense that Benoit was not expected to make it to the Beaumont show with either flight. There was also a twilight zone characteristic of the two timelines, whereby both were cited in some measure while being referred to as "the" timeline. For example, on Wednesday, June 27, Forbes.com would report that "the timeline" from WWE "states that on the afternoon of Saturday, June 23, Benoit, who was supposed to appear at a WWE event in Texas, contacted WWE to inform them that his wife and son were ill with food poisoning and he wouldn't make it. WWE rebooked his flight for Sunday morning." This combines elements of the first timeline (which mentions food poisoning but not a Sunday flight) with the second timeline (which mentions a Sunday flight and Nancy and Daniel being ill, but not food poisoning).

District Attorney Ballard also would contribute to the confusion between, and the fusing of, the two timelines. In his press conference at the crime scene on Tuesday, Ballard referred to "two" text messages from Chris to other wrestlers and talked about them in the context of Chris explaining that his family was sick. That was indeed the cover story Benoit put out in his Saturday phone conversations; however, it was not the content of his Sunday text messages.

The collective inconsistencies exceed the threshold of triviality. In particular, as we will see, they affect how Scott Armstrong's actions on Sunday morning are evaluated.*

The sheriff's report confirms the Saturday flight account. When Benoit "overslept" on Saturday morning — we now know he was actually prowling about a mansion containing one, or likely two, dead bodies — he missed his reservation on Delta Airlines Flight 1048 from Atlanta at 11:15 a.m. eastern time. (That ticket was issued out of Stamford, having been ordered through the WWE travel office.) He changed to a Delta flight departing at 5:27 p.m., but he missed that one, too, in the course of talking about his family emergency with Guerrero, Armstrong, and WWE Talent Relations; this aligns with Armstrong's reference, in the first timeline, to a flight arriving in Houston at 6:30 central time. Benoit's phone records and Delta Airlines' reservation records agree that he then made calls to Delta Member Services, and

---

* Would Benoit have been missed at a particular Houston hotel on Sunday morning or afternoon? The chaotic nature of WWE procedures for traveling talent suggests not. WWE wrestlers bear all out-of-pocket expenses and make their own arrangements for the regular tour events, known as "house shows"; some choose to stay in expensive hotels, while others cut corners in cheap motels. For TV tapings and pay-per-views, the WWE office does make more generous and plush arrangements, booking large blocks of rooms, often spread across more than one local hotel, in order to accommodate everyone from the front office, the TV personnel, the support crew, and the wrestlers (including a safe margin of backups to cover no-shows). Taking no chances, the company overbooks rooms in multiple locations, and neither the hotels nor WWE pay much attention to precisely who checks into which rooms where and when. The former are being paid handsomely to accommodate anyone and everyone associated with WWE. And the only thing the latter cares about is that the wrestlers "make their towns" and appear on time at the arenas.

according to Delta he booked himself onto Flight 4801 departing at 9:27 p.m.

There is no record of a Sunday morning flight.

WWE "house show" procedures call for the road agent to send the office a written rundown of how things went. In his report to the office on the Saturday night show in Beaumont, agent Dave "Fit" Finlay wrote: "We drove through a lot of storms. . . . It was 90-odd degrees, and all of a sudden the big storms hit. But nonetheless, we all made it, apart from Chris Benoit, who I guess had a little bit of family problems. So we reshuffled the card around a little bit." Benoit's scheduled opponent, Edge, grabbed the house microphone — in wrestling parlance, he "cut a promo" — and complained "that Chris Benoit was not here, and that he did not have an opponent, in addition to saying that no one is worthy of stepping into the ring with him." The entrance music for Ric Flair interrupted Edge. Surprise! Flair strutted down the aisle and became Edge's challenger in a match ending with a "schmazz" (an out-of-control brawl with outside interference), as Edge "stole" the win.

Fit Finlay concluded: "Just some smoke and mirrors to harden things up, and cover a heel finish on the end of a match that really wasn't supposed to happen."*

* * *

Early Sunday morning Benoit transmitted his infamous farewell text messages to Guerrero and Armstrong. Both

---

* The complete text of road agent Finlay's house show report to the WWE office, which I obtained via a company insider, is included in the companion disk. See "Order the DVD" at the back of this book.

of the WWE timelines and the sheriff's records are all in agreement about their timing and content:

> **4:53 a.m. eastern time in Georgia (3:53 a.m. central time in Texas) (Though not so identified in the timelines, this was obviously sent to both Guerrero and Armstrong. Subsequent messages on this list will be noted by eastern time only.)**
> From Chris's cell phone: *"Chavo, Scott. My physical address is 130 Green Meadow Lane, Fayetteville, Georgia. 30215"*
> **4:53 a.m. (to both Guerrero and Armstrong)**
> From Nancy's cell phone: *"The dogs are in the enclosed pool area. Garage side door is open"*
> **4:54 a.m. (to both Guerrero and Armstrong)**
> From Nancy's cell phone: *"Chavo, Scott. My physical address is 130 Green Meadow Lane. Fayetteville Georgia. 30215"*
> **4:55 a.m. (to both Guerrero and Armstrong)**
> From Nancy's cell phone: *"Chavo, Scott. My physical address is 130 Green Meadow Lane. Fayetteville, Georgia. 30215"*
> **4:58 a.m. (to Armstrong)**
> From Nancy's cell phone: *"Chavo, Scott. My physical address is 130 Green Meadow Lane. Fayetteville, Georgia. 30215"*

Yet according to WWE, Guerrero and Armstrong didn't make these messages known to company executives until 12:30 p.m. the next day. To put it charitably, the explanations for this thirty-hour gap are kaleidoscopic.

On July 18, 2007, Guerrero would tell Greta Van Susteren of Fox News that he didn't understand the messages and initially dismissed them as old or insignificant. Here is the relevant portion of the transcript:

> **VAN SUSTEREN:** *So he obviously didn't call you later that night [Saturday] to say, "I've arrived in Houston."*

GUERRERO: *He never arrived, right. Right.*

VAN SUSTEREN: *All right . . .*

GUERRERO: *He never arrived. I did get text messages from him, though, in the morning, early in the morning, about . . .*

VAN SUSTEREN: *Now, what time — let me ask you — I was just going to say, was the first — the time of the text message you received from him?*

GUERRERO: *If I remember correctly, it was 3:53 a.m. Houston time, which is 4:53 Atlanta time.*

VAN SUSTEREN: *And it said what?*

GUERRERO: *And that — yes, that text message said — it just had his address. He lived in — he'd just moved to this new house he had built because the last house that he had was kind of on a public — was on a public street, a public area, and he just couldn't go outside anymore. He was afraid for Daniel to be outside and playing because so many, you know, fans or people from the airport would just come and camp out in front of his house. So he couldn't really — he couldn't really have a public life anymore. So he went ahead and bought this land in suburban Atlanta, built the house out there and had a PO box, and no one really even knew his address. So those texts were — his — his — they were telling me what his physical address were. But nothing out of the ordinary, just, my physical address is this, and that's it. And he texted me again . . .*

VAN SUSTEREN: *Did he think that was peculiar, I mean, that — I mean, his address, was that odd?**

GUERRERO: *It was — you know, sometimes when you send a text and the person doesn't get that text until two days later, I*

---

* In a raw transcript, it can be difficult to determine exactly what the person is trying to say. Van Susteren here seems to be asking Guerrero what he thought Benoit was thinking. My investigation is more interested in what Guerrero himself was thinking at this point.

kind of — it was so early in the morning, I was sleeping. I looked at my text, and I'm going — I didn't know why he was sending that to me, so I thought maybe he sent it to me a day before or two days before or whatever, and I'm just getting it now. And then I got another text a couple minutes later saying, "The dogs are in the enclosed pool area and the garage door's open." I'm going — I didn't know if he was thinking that he wanted us to pick him up. But we were in Houston. I didn't really know what was going on. And so I thought again maybe it was a — just a text that was sent a couple — you know, a couple days ago. So I went back to sleep and . . .

VAN SUSTEREN: *I was going to say, was that the last text message you received from him?*

GUERRERO: *No, no. I received another one same — that was the same as the first one, My physical address is this (INAUDIBLE) this, whatever it was. That's — you know, it was the last text I got from him. And it was just — it was just so random. There wasn't a cry for help. There wasn't a, you know, "I love you." There was nothing in there. It was just kind of very, very random. So I didn't really think anything of it. I went back to sleep. And then in the morning, I kind of — I called him in the morning to see if everything was OK, but he didn't answer.*

VAN SUSTEREN: *And then when did you learn that he was dead?*

GUERRERO: *Not until the following day. That whole day was on Sunday. And we had a pay-per-view event. He was supposed to be at the pay-per-view event. He had a match. And it was very, very, very unlike him to miss the pay-per-view. He was really — didn't do that. To miss any match, he just — that never happened. Chris was the ultimate professional. And for him to miss a match was very strange. We were calling him all day and WWE was calling him. We were just trying to get a hold of him. We just never did until the next morning, when I mentioned to some of* *the WWE office that I got these weird text messages from him. So they sent a car out to his place, and I guess there was — the dogs were running around, so they couldn't really enter his house. And they said that the dogs were there, so they're trying to — they were trying to get into the house to find out what's going on, if anything — at that time, they didn't know what was wrong. So they had talked to me, and I told them that I think their neighbor, one of their neighbors knew them. So I think that's how they ended up getting in and finding what happened.*

Van Susteren didn't ask Guerrero why he made no connection between the texts and the strange "I love you" coda of his Saturday phone conversation with Benoit. Guerrero said the message was "just so random . . . [not] a cry for help" because there "wasn't a, you know, 'I love you.'" But the point of the "I love you" anecdote was not that collection of words per se, but the very quality that Guerrero targeted in the texts: their "randomness." So his insistence that the equally "random" texts should have elicited a cavalier response from him is hard to swallow.

Van Susteren also failed to ask Guerrero the key follow-up question: Even if he couldn't make heads or tails out of Benoit's text messages *when he first received them,* why would he have hesitated to share them with his bosses at WWE *after Chris failed to turn up for the pay-per-view on Sunday night?* By that point Benoit, in a complete break from his history of reliability, was missing not one, but two, nights of work amidst confusion about his whereabouts and the health of family members. Moreover, pay-per-views were special high-revenue events, and Benoit had a spot in a title-change match in this one.

Scott Armstrong's response to the text messages was even more perplexing. At 9:26 a.m. Sunday, a few hours after Benoit transmitted his final texts, Armstrong texted Benoit: "What time do u land?" Presumably Armstrong was referring to when an Atlanta-to-Houston flight would be touching down. It so happens that Armstrong's text is the only detail anywhere in the record reinforcing the notion, in the final WWE timeline, of a Sunday morning — rather than a Saturday night — flight.

The innocent implication of Armstrong's text was the chaos at that point surrounding all things Benoit. The more ominous implication is that he sent the message for the express purpose of corroborating the WWE story, retroactively concocted, that Benoit had been expected on a plane on Sunday morning. The second possibility is buttressed by the fact that Armstrong seemed not to know on what flight Benoit had allegedly been booked. Why would Armstrong drive to the airport cold, without getting the basic flight information from Benoit or from the WWE office?

When I first raised with sheriff's Detective Harper the contradictions suggested by Armstrong's Sunday morning text to Benoit, Harper said to me in a phone conversation, "That is very interesting." Later Harper emailed me, "The biggest point we took from the message is that it was unanswered. That helped with the timeline of when Chris died. There may have been a flight scheduled for Sunday, but that never came up in the homicide investigation. If the WWE scheduled the flight for him then they would be the best source for proof of the flight."

Still later, Harper maintained that when he had said "That is very interesting," he was referring only "to the way you were interpreting the text. During our conversation, I felt you were trying to say the text was planned or planted by Scott under some type of direction from the WWE." Harper did not clarify whether he agreed with the way he thought I was referring to the text.*

And as with Guerrero, this tidbit from Armstrong, even if honest, doesn't get us any closer to understanding why neither one of them told WWE about Benoit's texts when he remained missing in action at call time for the Sunday night pay-per-view.

Months after the media frenzy receded, Guerrero and Armstrong would simply ignore what Guerrero had told Greta Van Susteren about his initial reaction to the texts, and issue another version of why they didn't take action on Sunday. Benoit's wrestler friends were now telling colleagues that they had experienced cell phone reception problems in Texas; the messages were not received until Monday. They gave the same account to a television journalist working on the Benoit story. Dave Meltzer also heard this one.

"The Greta Van Susteren response is a very different explanation and makes even less sense because when Chris didn't arrive for the PPV, why didn't Chavo tell anyone?" Meltzer said. He added that at the time what Guerrero was saying on Fox News didn't seem that important, but now it does: "Again, if Chavo did get the text messages, why didn't he say anything to anyone until Monday?"

The fishiness of Guerrero's text message story gives

---

* Harper tied his afterthought remark to a false accusation that he had explained his "very interesting" remark in an earlier message, but that I had suppressed that explanation in my blog coverage. In fact, I had never received, and he almost certainly never sent, such an earlier message. For a full discussion of this controversy, see "Notes on Sources" at the end of this book.

fresh meaning to his behavior on Monday night at the *Raw* tribute. Chavo's on-camera messages that night were mixed. A five-minute testimonial, shot for WWE.com, shows Guerrero in tears. Between sobs, he manages these words:

> Chris Benoit was my friend, if not my best friend. He was part of my family, the Guerrero family. To tell you how close he was to my family and me, the night, the morning that I found Eddie, that Eddie died, the first one I called was Chris Benoit. And after telling him it almost broke my heart as much as finding Eddie, because to see a guy as hard as steel and chiseled and just a rock and never show emotion. And when I told him he wailed, he wailed and cried and was sobbing, was uncontrollable. Because Eddie was his best friend.

> The gift I was given when Eddie passed away was that I was able to be with him his last day and be the last one he saw. But I was given another gift because last week I spent the night at Chris Benoit's house. And — Chris never lets — he's a very private person. He doesn't let people in. And he let me in. He let me into his home, with his family and his dogs, fed me, put me up, made me feel at home. Then we went on a couple of house shows together, went to TV, went to dinner that next night, and we both missed our flights. I woke up to him banging on my door, "Come on, let's go, let's go, let's make your flight." He made it, just barely. I missed mine, but I was able to get home. He called to check up on me. I called to check up on him.

> And it's just . . . so hard to go through this again with someone I just respected so much as a person, as a friend, as a wrestler. . . . It was such a privilege and an honor to be in the ring with

him. I thank God for the actual matches we were able to have together, because they were some of the best of my career. I was able to learn so much from being in the ring with him. I remember, after we were done working together, I pulled him aside and thanked him, hugged him, told him I loved him, thank you so much for everything he's given me in the ring, in life. And we always left with a hug and a kiss and "I love you." That's something he didn't give out very willingly, he didn't give that to people, but we gave that to each other. And the last time I talked to him, the day before he passed, he ended the phone call with "I love you, Chavo."

I just want to say, Chris, you were my friend, I love you and you're part of my family. I don't say that about people, I say that about you. Thank you, God bless you, man. I feel for you. I feel for your family. I just — I'm so sorry. I thank you for the time we spent at *WrestleMania*, my kids and your kids, and they all played together. . . . The privilege and the trust you had in me, by letting me have your kids, I took them with my kids, and we went to the movies together. I guess that shows me how you thought about me, Chris. I thank you very much for that, for thinking of me that way, because I feel the same about you and I would trust you, with me, with my life, with my kids' lives, because I know you, Chris, I know your heart, and I know what a great heart you have — had, whatever. Thank you, Chris, and thank you for being my friend. Love you, man.

On the live *Raw* TV tribute show, however, Guerrero has a different demeanor, more like William Regal's; Chavo is detached, even shut down. In retrospect, colleagues thought Guerrero looked extraordinarily reserved for someone whose close friend had just died.

They figured that he may have suspected something, or just been confused.

* * *

On March 28, 2008, I called both Guerrero and Armstrong's cell phones. At the number for Guerrero, a male voice answered and, when I asked if he was Chavo Guerrero, replied, "Who are you?" I said, "Irv Muchnick" — whereupon the man said no, that he wasn't Chavo Guerrero and I had a wrong number. I later called back and got an outgoing message with the same voice. This was the same voice as the live one moments earlier, and it also sounded like the Chavo Guerrero on TV. I left a message, which was not returned.

At the number for Armstrong, a man answered and, before I could even identify myself, said he couldn't hear me. I called back and he repeated the exercise. I suspect he was feigning a bad connection, as everything sounded fine on my end on both calls. Later I called yet again, got voicemail, identified myself, and left a message, which was not returned.

Some months later a close friend of Armstrong's told me that he was at the Houston airport on Sunday morning when he texted Benoit "What time do u land?" If true, that would make some difference in the perception of Armstrong's actions. Specifically, it would go some distance toward suggesting that his Sunday text was not faked to support a phony timeline already under construction (as he could just as easily have transmitted a fake message from the comfort of his hotel room). That said, I do not know why Armstrong could not have told me himself that he went to the airport Sunday. And for the reasons stated, I am not convinced that he did.

Two timelines . . . a flight reservation on either Saturday night (early version) or Sunday morning (final version) . . . Benoit text messages that were either construed slowly (national TV interview) or clogged in the electronic pipeline (later private explanation). . . . Such details, on their face, are matters for resolution by law enforcement. District attorneys and sheriffs do not ordinarily close the files on heinous crimes without offering a coherent account of how and why three corpses lay undetected inside a house in their jurisdiction for more than thirty hours after the perpetrator, who was in the middle of missing important commitments for a high-profile job, sent five text messages to two colleague-friends. Indeed, failure or delay in reporting a crime is, itself, sometimes prosecuted as a crime, known as "misprision of a felony."

Yet closing the file without making any attempt to resolve these contradictions is precisely what Scott Ballard, the district attorney of the Griffin Judicial Circuit, and Randall Johnson, the sheriff of Fayette County, chose to do in the Benoit case. As will be shown in the next chapter, the authorities also airbrushed phone logs, concealed other text message evidence, retrieved no voicemail messages at all, and released a final report calculated to mislead in several other respects. They played shell games with public records, which cast them, and WWE, in a poor light.

Chris Benoit committed the crime all by himself. On general principle, we might settle for the murky final report on the murder-suicide with the resignation of Sheriff Tate in *To Kill a Mockingbird*, who says of the mysterious murder of bad guy Bob Ewell, "Let the dead bury the dead."

But the willful passivity of the Fayette County Sheriff's Office busted the buttons of that principle. To a public whose interest would be served by disclosure, not concealment, the local authorities did their best to stonewall facts about the modus operandi of the wrestling industry: its blurring of fact and fiction; its totalitarian control over talent, with no concern for safety, let alone honor; its resourcefulness at eluding scrutiny and projecting the right combination of imagery and bluster to ensure that business as usual would not be interrupted.

Unless those conditions are squarely faced and corrected, people will continue to die backstage, in numbers that dwarf the mortality rate of rock-and-roll stars, in the debris of ruthless big-money cartoons whose victims are merely replaceable parts without a constituency. Until then, future Chris Benoits are inevitable.

CHAPTER 8

The District Attorney, the Sheriff, and What's Missing

FAYETTE COUNTY HAD A CRIME PROBLEM, all right: stolen golf carts. In Fayette, recently built residential communities (such as Highgrove, near the Whitewater Creek Country Club, minutes from where the Benoits took residence in 2006), as well as entire charter municipalities (such as Peachtree City, where the Benoits had spent the previous nine years), were meticulously zoned and preplanned down to the last architectural, landscape, and lifestyle detail. The goals were comfort and stability. The unifying feature of most subdivisions — though the quaint suburban term "subdivision" itself seemed somehow beneath them — was a network of golf-cart paths, which proved equally congenial to pedestrians, baby strollers, and bicycles. The problem, from time to time, was that golf carts disappeared in clusters of either hardcore thefts or juvenile pranks. With each outbreak, the town pooh-bahs and the local newspaper, the *Citizen*, would brood over what to do about it.

Yes, there were also some gang issues in the schools, and Fayette County got its share of the heavy methamphetamine traffic throughout the region. But the bottom line was that Fayette encountered very little violent crime: around three and a half incidents annually per 1,000 people, in a total population of just over 100,000 — a rate half that of the state of Georgia as a whole. The Benoit murder-suicide was one of only two homicide incidents in the county in 2007.

This sylvan setting would have an impact on how the Benoit case was investigated. In exurbs far removed from mean streets, the worst fatalities in wrestling history, under the microscope of worldwide 24/7 media, taxed the capacity of public resources to administer them thoroughly and professionally.

Scott Ballard, who boasted multigenerational county roots, led the local law enforcement hierarchy. In 2004 Ballard was elected district attorney of the four-county Griffin Judicial Circuit. Beefy-faced, ruddy-complexioned, with a Senator Foghorn Leghorn white cowlick and a drawl as soothing as bourbon-and-branch-water, "Scooter," as he was known, continued to teach at his church Sunday school even as he hunted down the area's underwhelming criminal element Monday through Friday. Ballard mastered both the piety and the folksy political chops necessary to thrive in this enclave of dead-red Republicanism. When he ran for re-election in 2008, his opponent attempted to make an issue out of the fact that Ballard had agreed to testify as a character witness for a convicted child molester in a probation revocation hearing. Ballard won in a landslide anyway.

When the Benoit spotlight shone on Fayette County, Ballard was front and center, and he appeared intoxicated by it all. WWE lawyer Jerry McDevitt, who said he never spoke to the district attorney, accused Ballard of making "numerous public statements which were inappropriate and ultimately belied by the actual forensic evidence and failed to see to it that certain tests were done which might have supplied a motive and/or more complete picture of the circumstances within the Benoit family. Indeed, the disdain for Mr. Ballard is evident to anybody who speaks to the actual investigators."*

From the start, consciously or otherwise, Ballard stoked the frenzy, substituting attention-grabbing sound bites for measured words. A favorite trope was to label something "bizarre," a term made to order for splashy play. "The details, when they come out, are going to prove a little bizarre," he teased the media on the first day.

Ballard also said, "In a community like this it's bizarre to have a murder-suicide, especially involving the death of a seven-year-old. I don't think we'll ever be able to wrap our minds around this."

And: "Bizarre. That's the only way I can describe this."

And: "There was a Bible placed beside each of the bodies, and I thought that was somewhat bizarre."

And: "What's most bizarre to me is the timing and the circumstances. Not just that a man could kill his own seven-year-old son but that he could have stayed in the same house with the bodies."

Even as Ballard's serial proclamations of bizarreness fed the media beast, they contributed to slaking the thirst for concrete answers. Who cares about fissures in the back story — about multiple timelines and day-plus

---

* Presumably McDevitt referred only to public investigators, and the only one to whom I spoke was Detective Harper. "Disdain" may be strong, but when we talked about the evolution of news reports in the first hours, Harper insisted that any early leaks had to have come from the DA, not the sheriff's people.

gaps after text messages — when an obvious double murder-suicide can be written off as *sui generis* weird? As Forrest Gump might have put it, in Fayette County law enforcement, bizarre was as bizarre did.

* * *

Ballard's most reckless statement threw fat into the fire of what became either a fabricated forty-eight-hour distraction or a legitimate, though not exactly central, puzzle piece. That was the report that Daniel Benoit had a genetic disorder, Fragile X syndrome, which in turn gave rise to the theory — heavily promoted by WWE before being abruptly abandoned — that parental stress over Daniel's care drove Chris Benoit over the edge.

The Fragile X story established a pattern of the Benoit investigation and coverage: first, it surfaced in an exaggerated and irresponsible form; then, it was prematurely buried. Reviewing how the report found daylight makes it hard not to infer that it contained a germ of truth. Despite evidence that WWE — eager for anything that would turn the focus away from steroids — ran too hard and too fast with the Fragile X theory, the story itself appears to have been spontaneous, not planted.

Ballard got the ball rolling when he told the media that Daniel's arm showed needle marks from injections of growth hormone by his parents. The DA said he was told that Chris and Nancy were concerned about their son's size. "The boy was small, even dwarfed," Ballard said.*

---

* The Georgia medical examiner's report (referenced above, and included in the companion DVD) is, at most, silent on whether Daniel Benoit had

Nearly 3,000 miles to the northwest, a woman named Pamela Winthrope heard the news of the deaths in Georgia on a car radio tuned to Vancouver's News1130. The Benoit name rang a bell. Winthrope was an activist with the British Columbia chapter of the Fragile X Research Foundation of Canada, an organization raising funds and awareness for a syndrome that has been identified as the most common cause of inherited mental impairment and the most common known cause of autism. (Fragile X has a host of physical-development symptoms, as well, and differs widely among victims generally and between boys and girls especially.) Winthrope's son Jamie had Fragile X, and she was widowed. Before her husband died, she recalled his telling her that he had learned through the Fragile X community that the Benoits were also part of it, whereupon he contacted Chris Benoit about becoming a Canadian celebrity spokesman for the cause. Chris declined.

"I called the station to ask for more information," Pam Winthrope told me. "The person I spoke to [reporter Katharine Kitts] did not identify herself, nor did she tell me she was interviewing or recording. When I explained why I had called, she asked many questions about Fragile X. I, of course, am always happy to oblige."

Late the next day, Tuesday, June 26, Winthrope's daughter called to tell her that she was being quoted on the air by name, and it was all over TV and the Internet. In the on-air interview, which Winthrope said she did not authorize, she recalled her husband talking to Benoit

---

needle marks. If Dr. Kris Sperry intended to embed such an observation in ambiguous technical language, he wasn't saying.

"because I was trying to set up a support group in B.C. and in Canada, we only have a couple of them. My husband was struggling when we got diagnosed with our son, and Chris was struggling with his. They talked for a few minutes and then he said he didn't want to be a public face for Fragile X, he just wanted to keep it really, really quiet."

Winthrope complained to News1130 management that she had been ambushed. The station placated her with a second, extended interview focusing on Fragile X awareness.* Meanwhile, in the U.S., National Fragile X Foundation executive director Robert Miller issued an educational news release and found himself fielding questions from *People* magazine, TV's *Inside Edition*, and others; the foundation website had 30,000 visitors in three days, much more than the typical traffic of a busy month.

According to Winthrope, she never spoke with anyone from World Wrestling Entertainment. There is no reason to think she made up the story about Benoit and her late husband out of whole cloth. She was not a WWE stooge.

But once Winthrope's story got into the public domain, company spinmeisters did not pause to check out meticulously the state of Daniel's physical and mental health and its relevance to the double murder-suicide. At most, CEO Linda McMahon or her surrogates seem to have questioned some of Chris's friends, such as fellow wrestler Chris Jericho, who was in the midst of negotiat-

---

* Pam Winthrope exchanged emails with me in September and October 2007. The News1130 station manager, Jacquie Donaldson, refused to provide me with audio or transcripts, or to discuss the circumstances of Winthrope's two interviews. Reporter Katharine Kitts did not return messages.

ing his return to WWE after a period of inactivity. Jericho had seen the boy in social situations and, perhaps influenced by the power of retrospective impression, agreed that something must have been "off."

Jericho and others close to Chris Benoit also found authentic the idea that Pam Winthrope's husband would have been rebuffed in an effort to get Chris to go public about his own family's bout with a genetic disorder; that would be consistent with everything everyone knew about a man who looked as uncomfortable in his own skin outside the ring as he looked comfortable in it in the ring. In some Fragile X families, the shame and frustration of parents are said to be so profound that not even close relatives are told. If ever anyone fit such a profile, Benoit did.

And that, really, was all the confirmation WWE needed before putting its vast propaganda apparatus in motion. Thus, on the Wednesday, June 27, edition of *Good Morning America*, ABC's Robin Roberts introduced Linda McMahon by noting that "there are new clues surfacing that could take the case in a whole new direction — clues about a Benoit family secret: their seven-year-old son's rare genetic disorder, known as Fragile X . . . a point of tension between Benoit and his wife, apparently."

McMahon agreed. "The focus," she said, "is turning more to the tension that must have been happening between the husband and wife over the management, the schooling, and the rearing of this child who had the mental retardation."

In print media interviews, lawyer McDevitt reinforced the new message du jour. McDevitt said the couple's friends told WWE that Chris and Nancy had a hard time with Daniel's school placement. "I know that they had difficulty figuring out the solution and it was a cause of tension between the two of them." McDevitt said the Benoits "were constantly struggling with the difficulties of raising a child who, from all indications, may well have had Fragile X syndrome." He added, "It's very difficult to raise a child this way. There's a lot of guilt. Chris was traveling on the road, she was trying to deal with the problems on her own. . . . When they moved into this new area and the child had to be placed in a new district, I gathered the tension became somewhat exacerbated." McDevitt said that Daniel's special needs were part of a conversation Nancy had with Dr. Astin the previous Thursday, and that "we have reason to believe Chris talked about being depressed . . . with the situation."

By Tuesday, July 2, however, the tune was changing. After the attorney for the Toffoloni family, Richard Decker, insisted to ESPN that there was no record of Daniel having Fragile X, and that Daniel's grandparents had spent a lot of time with him and never noticed anything untoward, the DA backed off. Ballard issued this statement: "A source having access to Daniel's medical reports reviewed those reports. They don't mention any preexisting mental or physical impairment. Reports from Daniel's educators likewise contradict the claim Daniel was physically undersized. The educators report that Daniel graduated."

WWE took the cue. Spokesman Gary Davis said that while McDevitt had been "confident" in the accuracy of his earlier statements, "I think we have to go with what the district attorney has said as being the best up-to-date information available right now." A lot of people, Davis said, "got caught up in the idea that Daniel had Fragile X syndrome. We were just as caught up as everyone else."

McDevitt himself was more grudging; he either was

playing bad cop to Davis's good cop, or as a long-time trusted adviser to the McMahons, he had earned the independence to speak his own mind. McDevitt told *People* he had "reason to believe, and we believe the evidence will show, the situation with Daniel was a source of tension in the relationship between Chris and Nancy." And he continued to suggest that Chris's visit to Dr. Astin's Carrollton office on Friday was driven by a phone conversation the previous day in which Nancy discussed "the needs of the child and how they would be met," and that Chris talked in person with the physician about "the child and the family situation he was in."

Ballard, for his part, never bothered to resolve the contradiction between his original remarks and his reverse-field conclusion that Fragile X was a non-issue. The best guess is that the Toffolonis' unhappiness over the besmirching of Daniel's memory combined with Ballard's own belated perception that his indiscretion had served no positive purpose, since marital stress over a child's medical issues could never be posited as more than a minor part of this crime's equation.

Though Ballard did not grant an interview for this book, he did respond, in an email, to my questions to him about two anonymous posts at the time on the online discussion board of the *Citizen* newspaper. One of the posts said Ballard himself had a child with a challenge. Ballard confirmed, "My son, Paul, has autism." Another *Citizen* post asserted that, before Ballard was elected DA, he had represented some Atlanta-area wrestlers in his private law practice, though Benoit was not one of them. Ballard told me he handled some legal matters for Paul Orndorff and for Benoit's close friend Mike "Johnny Grunge" Dunham. Neither was with WWE at the time. (Orndorff had been a WWF main event star in the '80s. Dunham was with the company for two months in 1999.)

As for Daniel, the painful and counterintuitive truth was that he had been enrolled in a "bridge kindergarten" preschool class at First Baptist Church of Peachtree City. Such programs are designed for children who turn five years old right around the enrollment deadline for regular school kindergarten (typically late summer or early fall). That way, parents who aren't sure whether their borderline-age kids are school-ready can hedge their bets for a year; after the pre-K program, the kids are sent on to either kindergarten or first grade. But Daniel wasn't five, five and a half, or even six; he was seven.

On the *Citizen*'s discussion board, a poster identified only as "Christi" maintained, "Daniel did not have trouble dealing with other kids. He had lots of friends in his class. My daughter called him her boyfriend and said he used to protect her. He looked and acted like all the other kids in his class."

(Clearly a member of the pro-Nancy, anti-Chris faction, "Christi" also wrote: "The man did fake fighting in a ring with other men in tights. It's FAKE! They are all big muscular bad actors. Why does this qualify him as a hero??? It's WRESTLING!!! Chris had the personality of a wet mop. At least that's the impression my husband and I got from him at our kids' graduations. We also got a very bad vibe from him.")

Other sources close to the Toffolonis ascribed Daniel's enrollment at the First Baptist preschool to Chris's increasingly zealous desire to control Nancy and Daniel, and to a growing paranoia, which only lockdown security could satisfy. Chris talked a lot about the 2003 murder in the Atlanta area of the daughter of retired wrestler Khosrow Vasiri, "The Iron Sheik" — never mind that she was a grown woman who was killed by her boyfriend. The Benoits' move from Peachtree City to their gated home was motivated by safety concerns, as was the acquisition of the German shepherd guard dogs. During this period, Chris also began having a local hanger-on who drove him around, Jimmy Baswell, take different routes from the airport to home with the view of shaking off anyone who might be following them.

There's a difference, though, between being a control freak and a security fanatic, and making a school enrollment decision that would retard the academic career of a developmentally normal child. Juxtaposed against the known facts, the denials that Daniel had a medical condition came across as more defiant than convincing. Advocates of this viewpoint did not respond to my invitations to entertain follow-up questions.

The most telling sign that something was amiss with Daniel came from the authoritative, if muted, testimony of next-door neighbor Holly Schrepfer. Seeking to escape the June-July 2007 frenzy, Schrepfer traveled to the Boston area, where she'd previously lived. There Schrepfer, who had been a well-connected events producer, hired a Boston public relations firm, Regan Communications Group, to help her handle the barrage of media inquiries. George Regan issued a statement on Schrepfer's behalf acknowledging that Nancy Benoit, over the course of their year-long friendship, had spoken of Daniel's "medical problems." Regan said, "I know there were some problems, problems and issues that she said the son had."

The sheriff's report covers the subject by noting that

"rumors" about Daniel and Fragile X circulated during the investigation. "The rumors reported the Benoit family had a difficult time raising Daniel with this autism-like condition. Investigators with the Georgia State Composite Board of Medical Examiners obtained Daniel Benoit's medical records and were unable to locate any notation or evidence that Daniel Benoit suffered from Fragile X syndrome or any form of autism."

This conclusion would carry more weight if it included the medical records rather than a second-hand characterization of them, and if it had grappled with DA Ballard's statements about needle marks on Daniel's arm. If this was a false rumor with a fuse, Ballard was the one who lit it.

* * *

Not all the warps in the Fayette County investigation can be blamed on its loose-tongued DA. Some emanated from the sheriff's office. Others were by-products of combined and inglorious incompetence. These lapses may or may not have risen to the level of corruption.

Perhaps the most important such area was the authorities' baffling approach to the voice messages left on Chris and Nancy's cell phones. Home phone answering machine messages were captured, but those had little value; Chris, like most mobile people, communicated almost exclusively through his cell. From the primary-source audio of the voicemail left on that cell, we could backfill what others knew about the Benoits' crisis, or at least acquire hints of the levels of their concerns.

But the investigators did not retrieve any voicemail whatsoever. Moreover, they didn't even try.

A June 26, 2007, subpoena to Verizon Wireless Communications — submitted by DA Ballard and Detective Harper, and signed off on by a Fayette County judge — demanded documentation in fourteen categories. These included cell site activation, numbers dialed, incoming numbers, call duration, and incoming and outgoing text messages. Not one of the categories was incoming voicemail.

While discussing the voicemail issue for this book, Harper could not have been more vague or misleading. On April 5, 2008, I emailed Harper, in part, "Your report includes a printout of the text messages. Is it also technically possible to retrieve audio of the incoming voicemail messages? If so, was a demand for voicemail audio included in any of the 14 categories of the subpoena to Verizon? And did Verizon provide it? If audio of voicemail is not in the sheriff's records in this case, I would like to find out why."

Three days later, the detective responded, "Luckily, we were able to at least get the texts from the phones. We retrieved the data from the phones such as SMS (text messaging). We asked for them from Verizon, but due to an issue they had with their systems, they could only produce what they gave us and nothing more. They were unable to provide text or voicemails." Harper did not answer the question of whether a demand for voicemail audio was included in the Verizon subpoena, and I concluded that it was not. Harper also did not respond to the question of whether retrieving voicemail was technically feasible: the answer is obviously yes.

Below we will get to what the sheriff's office said about the text messages; for now, let's stick with voicemail. Harper was trying to combine the two under the heading of technical problems, when the bedrock reason for not obtaining the former was that it wasn't in the subpoena. He would not comment on what — or who — could possibly have persuaded him not to pursue this key evidence.

Assuming that the sheriff's office actually pressed Verizon informally for the voicemail — defective subpoena and all — but was told that the system was down, would Harper's explanation wash? Not according to the forensic experts I consulted, one of whom was Kevin Ripa of a company called Computer Evidence Recovery. "If there was a system error, then what about the backup system?" Ripa said. "Major telecommunications companies don't record mission-critical information casually. If Benoit's voicemail was truly missing for good, that is a serious problem that would have affected thousands of other customers, as well. Verizon surely could have been pressed further on this point."*

* * *

The sheriff's investigation did produce text messages, to and from both Chris and Nancy's cell phones; that evidence was especially useful in its depiction of their deteriorating marriage and her alarm over his drug use. Yet the text record, too, is incomplete.

On June 28, 2007, the *New York Daily News* reported that Chris had texted "biblical verses and portions of his will." No such messages would appear in the sheriff report's logs. Bryan Alvarez, publisher of the *Figure Four*

---

* Ripa's company, Computer Evidence Recovery (http://www.computerpi .com), is based in Calgary and, coincidentally, has done work there for the famous Hart wrestling family.

Weekly newsletter, echoed this report in an interview with National Public Radio the next day. "I've been told there are other messages that have not been made public yet that perhaps quoted biblical passages, had estate information. So I think more is going to come out as it pertains to the text messages," Alvarez said. When I followed up with Alvarez more than a year later, he said the report was probably just "confusion or some other miscommunication" in the first days.

On June 29, ex-wrestler Joe "Road Warrior Animal" Laurinaitis — brother of WWE Talent Relations chief John Laurinaitis — seemed to be telling Dan Abrams of MSNBC that John was among the recipients of the text messages from Benoit at the very end. No such messages are in the sheriff report's logs. However, in full context it is not clear whether Joe was merging unrelated pieces of already known information:

> [Y]ou better have a good reason [not to show up for a major booking] or your butt's getting canned. You're going to get fired. You know, my brother is vice president of operations for the WWE, my brother John. And I had — once I heard of this horrific situation, I called him and said, 'Man, what's going on?' He said *[and here is where the boundary between direct and indirect quotation gets jumbled]*, 'Man, all that I know is that some of the guys and my brother himself had got text messages saying, you know, this is my new address. The dogs are out on the deck. The side garage door's open' — just plain one-liners that didn't make any sense, that were so unlike Chris Benoit.*

---

* Joe Laurinaitis is the father of Ohio State's pro football–bound All-America linebacker, James Laurinaitis.

These tidbits do not prove the existence of suppressed texts. But at least one wrestler whose text messages appear on the log released by the sheriff told friends of other messages of his that mysteriously are not included.

The final piece fueling these strong suspicions has a tinge of Keystone Kops. In response to the subpoena, Verizon Wireless produced printouts of calls sent to and received by Chris and Nancy's cell phones. At the beginning of the printout is a legend with explanations of all the abbreviations and codes therein, and examples of how they were applied. One such example is the following text:

> **CTM data (ASCII)**
>
> [I don't understand any of this chris. What could ever have made u do this? U r a hero and my biggest influence in the bizness as well as my friend. But no]
>
> **Sent (ASCII)**
>
> [I don't understand any of this chris. What could ever have made u do this? U r a hero and my biggest influence in the bizness as well as my friend. But no]
>
> Originating Time [06/26/2007 02:51:15[00] [00001]

This text appears nowhere on the Verizon printout itself, much less on the sheriff report's logs. Could the author of the company's explanatory legend have gone to the trouble of making up such an elaborate hypothetical example, with this authentic-sounding voice and detail? (The sender of the message, real or imagined, would be someone who idolized Benoit and was in anguish upon learning that he was a murderer.) Highly, highly, highly doubtful.

True, a message mourning the family and posthumously judging Chris might have been excluded from the public record as "not relevant." In the February 12, 2008, records release, the sheriff hedged its incompleteness by calling the collection of text messages therein the "relevant" ones. But the authorities' definition of relevance seemed awfully crabbed and debatable — in a way that served WWE more than anyone legitimately scrutinizing it.

And anyway, the real point is that Verizon, in the official story, was supposed to have told Fayette County law enforcement that it could not produce *any* texts. According to the sheriff's report, Verizon's text data stopped at date, time, and phone number, with no content. Detective Shelton had to download from the Internet an open-source software called BitPim, with which he was able to access the text messages. So what's with the fully quoted example in the explanatory legend?

Later, when he got possession of the phones, Mike Benoit hired an expert to search for additional text evidence, but he never shared with me what, if anything, that exercise uncovered.*

* * *

The suspicion that the sheriff reported the telephonic evidence in bad faith is slam-dunked by the discrepancies between the raw phone call logs produced by Verizon and the final sanitized logs created by the sheriff. The public Benoit investigation report released the latter with the subtle suggestion that they were

---

* The sheriff report's version of the text message logs is included in the companion disk. See "Order the DVD" at the back of this book.

comprehensive. Though no disclaimer language was included to inform readers that calls documented by Verizon had been deleted, this secondary, interpretive log produced by the sheriff abruptly stops listing calls to Chris Benoit's cell phone after 1:34 p.m. Sunday — more than twenty-four hours before the bodies were discovered. Again, the only defense for this would be the dubious contention that subsequent calls were "not relevant." Why was 1:34 relevant but not 1:35, or 5:52, or 8:00 (which was bell time for the *Vengeance* pay-per-view)?

Detective Harper, Sheriff Johnson, and DA Ballard all ignored repeated inquiries about the incomplete cell phone call logs. In emails from Richard Lindsey, the attorney representing the sheriff's office, he expressed the legalistic view that the Georgia open records statute did not require public agencies to explain or justify why they did not produce something different than what they released, despite what a critic could argue were fundamental inconsistencies.

The sheriff's logs' known omissions of phone calls on the Benoits' several phone numbers include five calls made by WWE executive John Laurinaitis on Sunday after Chris killed himself: 4:27, 4:46, and 6:25 p.m. (before the Houston pay-per-view show), 8:25 (during the show), and 11:56 (afterward). There were numerous other calls from WWE cell phones, plus two others from cell phone numbers in Stamford, the company's headquarters city.

In addition, there were the following calls:

- 4:21 p.m. from a cell phone in Florida — perhaps Dean Malenko, a WWE agent and Benoit's old "Three Amigos" pal.

• 4:32 from a land line in California — most likely wrestler Oscar "Rey Mysterio" Gutiérrez.

• 4:40 from Scott Armstrong. Interestingly, this call adds additional weight to the theory that Armstrong, a recipient of Benoit's early morning texts, truly believed that his friend would be on an Atlanta-to-Houston plane that morning, and that Armstrong might even have been at the airport waiting for Benoit at 9:27 a.m., when Armstrong texted, "What time do u land?" (The alternative theory is that the Armstrong text — perhaps even if accompanied by Armstrong's drive to the airport — along with this afternoon call by Armstrong, simply had the purpose of contriving a timeline item. But, as noted earlier, the alternative theory is somewhat weakened if Armstrong went to the trouble of driving to the airport.)

• 4:43 and 6:26 from a WWE cell phone. If there was a one-digit typo in the printout, it is possible that this was from the same person, "Mark," who would text Benoit on Monday a willingness to "kayfabe for you" if Benoit was in any kind of trouble. (One of John Laurinaitis's assistants in talent relations was named Mark Carano, but would not qualify as someone in the WWE inner circle of top executives.)

• 7:50 from a phone at the Toyota Center in Houston.

• Several calls from Canada — from an old workout buddy of Benoit's and from his ex-wife, Martina.

• Perhaps significantly, no apparent calls from Chavo Guerrero. This raises the possibility that Guerrero and Scott Armstrong did not have the same level of information, even though both were recipients of the same early-morning texts;

or, if they did have the same information, they acted different-
ly on it, either in separate decision-making or in coordination.

* * *

WWE lawyer McDevitt and I agree on at least one thing:
the performance of the district attorney was very poor.

"In point of fact, the authorities did not do many
things which should have been done, and which they
were urged to do, and did several things which should
never be done in any competent investigation," McDevitt
wrote in an email complaining about my blog coverage.
"Foremost among such actions was releasing the crime
scene, together with critically important evidence, to
persons with financial interests within a day of discovering the bodies. Indeed, it is a matter of historical record
that I called on authorities during a national television
program to locate Chris Benoit's diary when I learned of
it since it might have shed light on the murders.
Incredibly, when it finally was located or retrieved, it was
evidently given to Michael Benoit rather than maintained in police custody."

McDevitt's account of the diary debacle is substan-
tially accurate. Ballard's decision to allow Nancy's side of
the family to move into the house almost immediately,
and thereby to gain special access to the crime scene, was
the crown on the DA's comedy of errors.

Whether with the goal of concealing secrets or merely
in an incoherent homicidal mania, Chris appeared to
have thrown a number of items into an outside trash
container.[*] One of the items was the diary Chris began

---

* Interestingly, drugs were not among the things Benoit might have keeping after Eddie Guerrero's death. Apparently, the cops missed the diary, either inside the house or in the trash can; if the former, then the Toffolonis might have attempted to dispose of the diary, perhaps because it was simply too unpleasant to confront in their grief, or perhaps because it would strengthen the case of Chris's side of the family that he suffered from dementia and was not responsible for his actions.

From what we know, the diary includes rambling biblical references, as well as passages directly addressed to Guerrero in the beyond. (If the *Daily News* report of the former in unreleased text messages was inaccurate, that could explain where that piece of confusion originated.) The only glimmer of the content, other than excerpts read by Mike Benoit in broadcast interviews, came in Chris's email exchanges with journalist Greg Oliver after Guerrero's death. "My wife Nancy bought me a diary and I have started to write letters to Eddie. It may sound crazy but that is how I'm coping," Chris wrote to Oliver.

On a visit to Chris and Nancy's house, some time after authorities released it to the Toffolonis, next-door neighbor Holly Schrepfer is believed to have retrieved the diary and then given it to Mike Benoit.

In our exchanges, McDevitt took exception to a quote in my blog coverage from an unnamed source who stated that WWE had played the Fayette County authorities "like a cello." That phrase was uttered by Patricia Roy, one of Mike Benoit's lawyers. To the extent that

---

discarded. This led some to theorize that one of his last conscious acts was to countermand the standard wrestler's practice of getting rid of a dead wrestler's drugs. In this way, the theory goes, he hoped to keep one of the root causes of his rampage from being covered up.

McDevitt wanted to highlight that the work of the authorities had been incompetent, and to argue that the incompetence had as much of a claim to the explanation of the gaps in the record as corruption, he may have had a point. In the end, we don't know *why* the Fayette County district attorney and sheriff screwed up the investigation of the thirty-hour text message gap, and not knowing why includes not knowing if they were in someone's pocket. We only know that they did screw up.

In an age of instant and unverified information, the only element missing from this tableau of mind-bending ambiguity would be an excruciatingly intriguing Internet rumor, transmitted through the ether and never pinned down, but nonetheless shedding additional light on WWE's preposterous timeline and the lengths to which the company went to divert attention from it.

And guess what? Thanks to the "Wikipedia hacker," the Benoit case had that element, too.

Chris Benoit got his start in Calgary-based Stampede Wrestling.

STAMPEDE WRESTLING

TUESDAY, OCTOBER 11—7:30—EX. AUDITORIUM

STREET FIGHT!
SPECIAL REFEREE—BRUCE HART

JOHNNY SMITH
-vs-
CHRIS BENOIT

INTERNATIONAL TAG TEAM CHAMPIONSHIP
CUBAN COMMADOS -vs- LANCE IDOL—BRUCE HART

JASON THE TERRIBLE -vs- GARRY ALBRIGHT
RIP ROGERS -vs- STEVE BLACKMAN
LEO BURKE -vs- GREAT GAMA

NEW! ADVANCE TICKET SALES AT AGRIDOME BOX OFFICE
ADULTS: $8 ADVANCE—$9 AT DOOR
SENIORS & 17 OR UNDER: $6 ADVANCE—$7 AT DOOR

Good Lookin' **STV** CHANNEL 11/CABLE 5

WATCH "STAMPEDE WRESTLING"
Good Lookin' STV-Channel 11—Cable 5
SATURDAY AFTERNOON

Benoit idolized the wrestler known as the Dynamite Kid (above, flying). The Kid (Tom Billington) is now crippled and broke in his native England.

Nancy Toffoloni was a bikini model who hooked up with Championship Wrestling from Florida as "Fallen Angel," the valet for Kevin Sullivan (top left), whom she married. Nancy later was "Woman" in World Championship Wrestling, where she and Chris turned a TV skit into reality.

Nancy and Chris strike a loving pose.

Chris's reckless style and athletic precision turned him into a WWE champion and one of the world's most popular and highest-paid wrestlers.

Chris Benoit and Eddie Guerrero (right) were soul mates. Guerrero's November 2005 death devastated Benoit.

Johnny Grunge (below, left) was the last Peachtree City wrestling friend with whom Benoit remained close. Like Benoit, Grunge was a patient of Dr. Phil Astin, who would later plead guilty and begin serving a ten-year prison term for overprescribing drugs. Grunge died three months after Eddie Guerrero, and Benoit sank into seclusion and paranoia.

The Signature Pharmacy list . . .

Batista   Booker T   Simon Dean   Edge

Funaki   Charlie Haas   Shane Helms

Ken Kennedy **Chris Masters** **Santino Morella** **John Morrison**

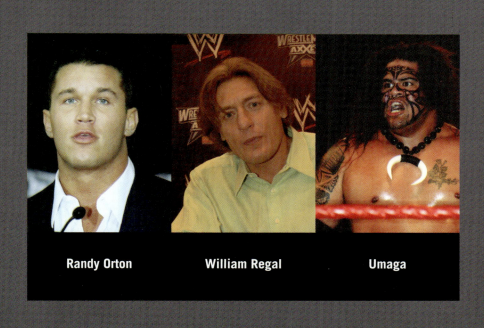

Randy Orton **William Regal** **Umaga**

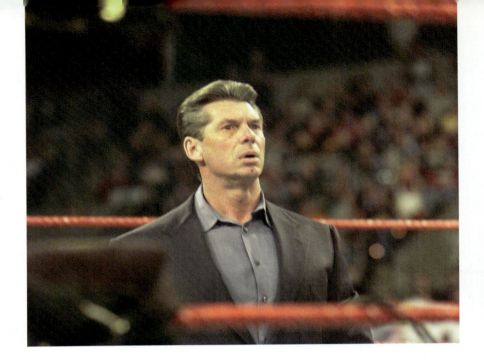

Vince McMahon, chairman of WWE, made the call to turn the Monday night wrestling show on the USA cable network into a tribute to Benoit — hours after the head of WWE Canadian operations told Benoit's father that the Georgia authorities knew Chris had murdered his wife and son and killed himself.

Nancy suspected Chris of carrying on an affair with a WWE diva. Text message evidence and other sources indicate that the diva was Michelle McCool.

TV news crews and wrestling fans flocked to the Benoits' Federal-style house on seven acres just outside Fayetteville, Georgia.

Chris's appointment book, maintained by Nancy, open to the page showing his appearance in Dothan, Alabama, where they had a confrontation leading to their final blow-up.

Wrestler Chavo Guerrero (left, punching) and ex-wrestler and referee Scott Armstrong (right) gave conflicting accounts of Chris Benoit's final text messages to them early Sunday morning. According to WWE's published timeline, company officials were not made aware of them until Monday afternoon.

Wrestler David Taylor (left; pictured here with Paul Burchill), who lived in Fayette County and at the time worked for WWE, was near the crime scene with his wife and another woman, carrying plates of food. The Taylors talked to the Benoits' next-door neighbor moments after she and sheriff's deputies discovered the bodies.

An Associated Press story erroneously stated that Chris Benoit's Wikipedia page mentioned Nancy's death before Chris's final text messages were received. Lawyer Jerry McDevitt was the main WWE source for the AP report. McDevitt also told the media that "none" of the drugs found in the Benoit house "came from Internet pharmacies." But some had the label of a Chinese company, and investigators immediately announced that Benoit was on the customer list of Internet gray-market dealer Signature Pharmacy.

District Attorney Scott Ballard fed the Benoit media frenzy with sensationalized statements. In particular, Ballard initially stoked the story that seven-year-old Daniel Benoit was "dwarfed" and had been injected with growth hormone. A woman in Vancouver spontaneously emerged to say that her late husband had talked with Chris Benoit about becoming a spokesperson for families of children with a condition called Fragile X Syndrome.

Former wrestler Chris Nowinski, whose career was ended by concussions, championed the theory that Chris Benoit's occupational brain trauma was responsible for his homicidal behavior.

Congressman Henry Waxman's committee threatened but did not hold public hearings on pro wrestling. Instead, the committee staff interviewed Vince McMahon and others behind closed doors, and didn't release the transcripts for more than a year.

In 2009, the governor of Connecticut named Linda McMahon, Vince's wife and the CEO of World Wrestling Entertainment, to the state Board of Education.

Daniel Benoit's toy championship belt lies on the floor next to the bed in which his father murdered him.

CHAPTER 9

The Wikipedia Hacker

SOONER OR LATER ANY PROBE of pro wrestling's mysteries crawls into a bunny hutch of surrealism, a tunnel of barbershop mirrors with no way out. Call it an alternative universe, or a place where fantasy imposes its will on truth, or just call it a weave of meta-events too tangled to unravel. In the Chris Benoit double murder-suicide, that bunny hutch is the strange tale of the nineteen-year-old Stamford, Connecticut, college student who posted on Wikipedia the news of Nancy Benoit's death, fourteen hours before the authorities knew of it.

It would be folly surpassing that of young Matthew T. Greenberg himself, the now-iconic "Wikipedia hacker," to suggest that this angle does or ever could answer the biggest questions of the Benoit investigation; the official findings of the crime and its perpetrator remain intact regardless. On the other hand, if the Wikipedia story meant nothing at all, then why couldn't the principals who looked into it have stopped sashaying long enough to lay out the handful of objective, non-self-referential facts that would easily establish its purportedly innocuous nature?

Assuming the explanation is entirely innocent — a reasonable hypothesis though, when it comes to wrestling, never a completely safe one — then the attendant dissembling could be written off to muscle reflex. Muscle reflex on behalf of the privacy of an essentially harmless prankster who learned his lesson about the dangers of monkeying around on the computer, and who stumbled onto the worst possible prank in the worst possible way. That, plus the "kayfabe" muscle reflex of the carnies who were, for once, victims of a hoax rather than its perpetrators, but who don't like to disclose their inner workings under any conditions.

In Greenberg's case, however, the temptation to dismiss the story is leavened by knowledge that World Wrestling Entertainment might have had a specific motive for keeping the Wiki fiasco under wraps. The more the public was exposed to even an honestly misguided suggestion that someone had gotten a premature tip about one or more Benoit family deaths, then the more people might reflect on the unbelievable thirty-hour gap between when Chris Benoit sent Chavo Guerrero and Scott Armstrong the final text messages and when the timeline insists "WWE officials" were informed of them. Once the Matthew Greenberg cat got out of the bag — whether wildcat or pussycat, it didn't matter — WWE's credibility firewall, in the form of two similar-but-different timelines, was in danger of being breached. It's a lot easier for corporate PR to justify a crisis response that was triggered Monday afternoon rather than early Sunday morning.

Greenberg therefore represented somewhat more than a brief, perhaps unintended, center of attention during the media frenzy. He was also someone whose consequences the powers-that-be had to work overtime to suppress, for they wanted to make sure he didn't wind up getting elevated to the status of the Benoit story's answer to Brandon, the young fan in the 1999 movie *Galaxy Quest*. In that parody of *Star Trek*, Brandon has encyclopedic knowledge of his cult, which comes in handy for the climactic solution finally figured out by Tim Allen's character, a washed-up and cynical former actor on the TV show. The verisimilitude of *Galaxy Quest* has such a hold on the sweet, hollow souls of its followers that it has inspired the architecture of an entire civilization in another quadrant of the universe.

* * *

This much is known: Late in the night of Sunday, June 24, 2007, an anonymous poster logged on to Wikipedia from a computer with the Internet Protocol (IP) address 69.120.111.23, via Cablevision's Optimum Online service provider.

The Wiki page with the biography of Chris Benoit had already been edited, at 10 p.m. eastern time, to note, "Chris Benoit was replaced by Johnny Nitro for the ECW Championship match at Vengeance, as Benoit was not there due to personal issues." A minute past midnight Monday, eastern time, poster 69.120.111.23 added at the end "stemming from the death of his wife Nancy."

Strictly speaking, this edit was not a "hack," nor even necessarily a hoax. Billing itself as "the free encyclopedia that anyone can edit," Wikipedia, launched in 2001, amalgamates information from a network of more than 15 million global users. More than 130,000 of these are active volunteer editors, around 100,000 of them in the English language. Serving as virtual gatekeepers is a force of more than 1,600 "admins" (administrators), who play catch-up in the vetting of facts published in real time in a bank of articles, long and short, which in 2009 surpassed the three million mark. In the sense that "hacking" is a generic term — used by the technologically challenged to describe a range of crude acts by those who are more comfortable with computers and exploit that skill gap for nefarious ends — the word is appropriate.

According to Wikinews, a Wikipedia affiliate, the Benoit edit by 69.120.111.23 was reversed "just under one hour later with the [admin's] comment: 'Need a reliable source. Saying that his wife died is a pretty big statement, you need to back it up with something.'"

The Wikinews report continued: "Then just one hour after the first edit reversion, another anonymous edit by 125.63.148.173 using *unwiredAustralia.com.au,* a wireless Internet service provider, was made about the aforementioned personal issues: '*which according to several pro wrestling websites is attributed to the passing of Benoit's wife, Nancy.*'" That edit, too, was quickly reverted with the comment: "Saying 'several pro wrestling websites' is still not reliable information."

One of the many online wrestling forums buzzing with Benoit news and gossip was one called Smart Marks. At 11:18 Monday night, Jonathan Barber, a Smart Marks poster with the handle LucharesuFan619, claimed credit for being the first person to trace the IP address 69.120.111.23 and notice that the Wikipedia edit had come from Stamford, the home of WWE.

The next day the Wikimedia Foundation's volunteer coordinator, Cary Bass, notified the Georgia authorities. Bass said someone put the pieces together "and realized that the comment was made by someone who apparently knew about the murders." On Thursday major news outlets broke the story of how the police were working on the mystery of an explosively curious Benoit edit on Wikipedia.

That night, at 12:26 a.m. eastern time Friday, 69.120.111.23 confessed in another anonymous post, on the "talk" page of Wikinews:

> Hey everyone. I am here to talk about the wikipedia comment that was left by myself. I just want to say that it was an incredible coincidence. Last weekend, I had heard about Chris Benoit no showing Vengeance because of a family emergency, and I had heard rumors about why that was. I was reading rumors and speculation about this matter online, and one of them included that his wife may have passed away, and I did the wrong thing by posting it on wikipedia to spite there being no evidence. I posted my speculation on the situation at the time and I am deeply sorry about this, and I was just as shocked as everyone when I heard that this actually would happen in real life. It is one of those things that just turned into a huge coincidence. That night I found out that what I posted, ended up actually happening, a 1 in 10,000 chance of happening, or so I thought. I was beyond wrong for posting wrongful information, and I am sorry to everyone for this. I just want everyone to know it was stupid of me, and I will never do anything like this again. I just posted something that was at that time a piece of wrong unsourced information that is typical on wikipedia, as it is done all the time.
>
> Nonetheless, I feel incredibly bad for all the attention this got because of the fact that what I said turned out to be the truth. Like I said it was just a major coincidence, and I will never vandalize anything on wikipedia or post wrongful information. I've learned from this experience. I just can't believe

what I wrote was actually the case, I've remained stunned and saddened over it.

I wish not to reveal my identity so I can keep me and my family out of this since they have nothing to do with anything. I am not connected to WWE or Benoit at all in anyway. I am from Stamford as the IP address shows, and I am just an everyday individual who posted a wrongful remark at the time that received so much attention because it turned out to actually happen. I will say again I didn't know anything about the Benoit tragedy, it was a terrible coincidence that I never saw coming.

I hope this puts an end to this speculation that someone knew about the tragedy before it was discovered. It was just a rumor that I had heard about from other people online who were speculating what the family emergency Chris was attending to. I made a big mistake by posting this comment on his page, since all we had were what we thought was going on and nothing about what actually was going on yet, and sadly what happened turned out to be my speculation at the time. I assumed wiki would edit out my information, which they did, so thats why I didn't go back to edit it out myself.

I know I keep repeating it but I feel terrible about the mainstream coverage this has received, since it was only a huge coincidence and a terrible event that should of never happened. I am not sure how to react, as hearing about my message becoming a huge part of the Benoit slayings made me feel terrible as everyone believes that it is connected to the tragedy, but it was just an awful coincidence. That is all I have to say, I will never post anything here again unless it is pure fact, no spam nothing like that. Thank you, and let this end this chapter of the Benoit story, and hopefully one day we will find out why this tragedy ever actually happened.

In subsequent exchanges on the talk page, 69.120.111.23 was asked if he would grant an interview. He replied:

Hey, I'm sorry but I would prefer not to do an interview, I really just want to put all this behind us. I made a mistake and I'm sorry, I know I've said that a million times but today has just been a bad day with this getting all this mainstream coverage even though it was just a huge coincidence. If an interview is deemed necessary, than I will only do it under the condition that I remain anonymous out of respect for my privacy. But really I would rather not do one, all that needs to be known is that this situation was blown out of proportion, though I can understand why.

I'm just still in shock that what I posted turned out to be true, and I feel awful that my post turned into a huge story, when it was only speculation on my part. Sorry I'm writing a lot, I just want to move on from this mistake and I hope you understand this. Thank you.

I also want to clarify again that the comment wasn't meant to be a prank, but just speculation on my part from some rumors that I had heard on the internet about the family emergency that caused Chris to miss the pay per view Vengeance. It was stupid of me to post, and I regret it, but I did and that won't change, but as long as everyone knows that it was simply a coincidence and nothing more then we can move on from this. Also, I'd like to apologize for my other wiki "updates" on other pages as they were immature and dumb, but I know I'm not the only one who has done this, but nonetheless I will never post anything like that again as I have learned from this. Thank you again.

By this time, online journalist Corey Spring was already putting the finishing touches on an investigation of the Wikipedia affair, which he would post at 3:04 a.m. on his page on another website called Newsvine. Spring found that 69.120.111.23 had also been responsible for several other Wikipedia alterations dating back to May 16 of that year. At the Wiki page for the city of Naugatuck, Connecticut, for example, he replaced the name of the town's mayor and other officials with those of three friends; reporter Spring's research on the social-networking sites MySpace and Facebook revealed that they were all part of a circle of students at the University of Connecticut in Storrs.

Furthermore, 69.120.111.23 had been warned in the past for vandalizing content and for posting pranks displaying a range of immature behavior. On the page of Stacy Kiebler, an actress and former wrestling personality, he wrote: "People want to @!$%# her in her lovely @!$%# and whip her ass til the dawn of day. Many people fantasize about ramming their cocks up her @!$%#." On the page of Ron Artest, 69.120.111.23 called the basketball player "a piece of @!$%# nigger!!!!!!!" (Though Spring did not clarify this, his report appeared to be cleaning up the epithets with the same series of characters for each one.) 69.120.111.23 replaced the Wiki page of information about the African Wild Ass with one word: "piss."

There was one out-of-character Wikipedia edit by 69.120.111.23, on the page of Chavo Guerrero. On the evening of June 15, 2007, someone else had inserted: "Before starting his wrestling career, Chavo was addicted to crack and was a rapist. One day when Chavo was doing crack he thought he saw a little white kid but it was actually his son, and sexually abused him until his penis fell off. On this day forth he will no longer rape his kid, but he still rapes people (even though he has no penis) so watch out for him, even adults." Three hours later, 69.120.111.23 went onto the page and deleted this vulgar, defamatory material. It was the Benoit hacker's only known instance of benign editing.

* * *

On Friday morning, June 29, Stamford police called the Greenberg house in the Stamford East Side's Cove neighborhood and spoke to Matthew's father, Steven Greenberg, who worked for the City of Stamford Finance Department. From information provided by Comcast/Optimum Online, the Fayette County Sheriff's investigators had traced the Wikipedia edit to Matthew Greenberg and asked Stamford to assist. Steven took Matthew to police headquarters. At 1:35 p.m., Detective Tim Dolan questioned Matthew in an interrogation room at the Bureau of Criminal Investigations.

The friendly interview lasted less than twenty-five minutes. Detective Dolan did not ask a single question about Chavo Guerrero.

Matthew Greenberg called himself a "pretty big" wrestling fan who, starting around 10 p.m. Sunday, "was reading rumors and speculation online" about Benoit missing *Vengeance*, perhaps because "his family was sick and someone maybe died, like his wife perhaps." But it was "more of my speculation." He didn't know about the three deaths until he returned Monday night from his summer job at Bed Bath & Beyond and saw the announcement on the front page of WWE.com.

Where online had he read the rumors on Sunday night? Dolan asked.

"Like, on forums. I forgot the exact, like, sites."

The detective wasn't too concerned about Greenberg's faulty memory of his involvement in world-news events less than five days earlier. The forensic specialists who would analyze Greenberg's laptop computer, Dolan said confidently, will "find out where these rumors started. . . . As long as you were in [a particular website] and looked at it, they can check it."

Greenberg said, "I totally — I kind of forgot I posted the Wikipedia thing. I didn't even think about that. Then, like, last night I was hearing about it and I posted, like, an apology in a Wikinews article. I just wasn't really sure how to react. I was probably going to call, like, the police soon, because I felt so bad. It was such a huge coincidence."

Steven Greenberg, the father, interjected to ask if there were any other posts saying Nancy had died.

"His was the only post!" Dolan said. He was wrong. There was also the second edit from Australia, which somewhat more responsibly cited as its source "several wrestling websites." The authorities never pursued that one. For what it's worth, the syntax of the very first edit, which was accurate and was retained by the Wiki editors, ended with a dependent clause beginning with "as," sounding more like British or Australian English than the most common usage in either the U.S. or Canada.

The detective started to leave the room to get a consent form for the computer search, and the father asked if Matthew was in trouble. Dolan said probably not. The elder Greenberg then said, without prompting, "I was thinking because he's from Stamford. . . . We live around the corner from them [WWE office], almost."

Incredibly, Dolan had not even brought up this subject. Now he said: "Well, I'm sure there was some of that. That's what I thought originally, but then I talked to the, uh. . . ."

Steven Greenberg interrupted him, and Dolan never finished the thought. Instead of explaining who had persuaded him that Matthew had nothing to do with WWE, the detective turned back to scold him. "To be honest, this isn't the first time you've adjusted a site. . . . Didn't you change the name of a mayor of a town to a couple of your friends?" Watch it, he warned, "You can turn yourself from a prank to a murder suspect" with that kind of stuff.

Dolan proceeded to pin down Matthew's alibis during the Georgia murders — he'd hung out with a couple of friends in New Rochelle, New York, on Friday night and was home all of Saturday and Sunday.

Dolan never got around to Stacy Kiebler and Ron Artest.

* * *

If the Stamford detective's softball interrogation was predicated on the expectation that the computer forensic exam would reveal the websites young Greenberg had visited, that expectation proved to be misplaced. Stamford police farmed out the exam to Detective Chester Perkowski of the nearby Darien police. Perkowski didn't waste a lot of breath in his report. "An examination of the computer's hard drive revealed no information about the homicide that was posted prior to June 25, 2007," he wrote.

When I spoke to Detective Perkowski more than a year later, it was apparent that he didn't know Chavo Guerrero from Chita Rivera. If Fayette County had asked Stamford — and Stamford in turn had asked Darien — to find the evidence on Greenberg's computer of where he had picked up on Nancy Benoit death rumors, Perkowski had not internalized the message. He told me he felt that his mandate was simply to find out if there was any evidence on the computer linking Greenberg to the crime. And there was none. Period.

Perkowski acknowledged that the computer showed some Internet history but said it was insignificant and not worth citing in his report. He added that it was possible that Greenberg, like many computer users, had used software to wash off traces of sites he had browsed.

Forensics expert Kevin Ripa of Computer Evidence Recovery said that explanation was bunk. "Most history-scrubbing software is a joke," Ripa said, adding that he had consulted on cases "where files were not only cleansed, but also allegedly deleted altogether, and I was still able to recover data. If the Connecticut report couldn't recover data, it at the very least could have recovered evidence confirming that scrubbing software had indeed been used."

* * *

Wikipedia founder Jimmy Wales had told the media, "The guy who's admitted to doing it said it was just a coincidence. He said he was hearing rumors. I wonder where those rumors came from. I guess the police will figure that out eventually." But the police never figured it out and never seriously tried. The media likewise turned the page on the "coincidence." Nearly eight months later, the Fayette County sheriff's report was released.

In a supplemental attached to the main report, Detective Josh Shelton wrote, "Det. Tim Dolan informed me after the interview that Matthew was simply speculating as to the reason Benoit missed the event and described Greenberg as 'harmless.'"

The main body of Detective Harper's report devoted far less space to the Wikipedia edit than to information wwe had provided, early on, about activity at a wwe.com chat room starting at 9:41 p.m. Sunday. There a user who called himself "GOB_The_Illusionist" typed, "Benoit's wife died." Another, "MaggieCrumb," responded, "Woman is gone!" GOB_The_Illusionist came back with, "Benoit killed his wife," and "_JUPITER" agreed: "benoit killed his wife."

The chat room chatter continued:

> _JUPITER: *"benoits wife is eead"*
>
> _JUPITER: *"dead"*
>
> GOB_The_Illusionist: *"ChrisBenoit is a murderer."*
>
> uk_batista_uk: *"where u read benoits wife is dead?"*
>
> _JUPITER: *"dave meltzer reported benoit is suspected for killing his wife"*
>
> buster: *"benoit has family problems"*
>
> uk_batista_uk: *"whos dave meltzer"*
>
> GOB_The_Illusionist: *"Benoit killed his wife like that nigger. In Ohio"*
>
> Fighting_Rules: *R.I.P. benoits wife?*
>
> Lilkenny: *benoits wife died??*
>
> Spanked_Monkey: *benoit is dead?*
>
> LitaKD: *Is Benoits wife really dead??*
>
> CmPunkfan2007: *BENOITS WIFE DIED?*
>
> Philgr: *R.I.P. BENOITS WIFE*

GOB_The_Illusionist was found to be Sheldon Chandler, a fan in Orlando, Florida. "Some people was really trying guess why he wasn't there," the guy explained in an email to Shelton, "but some were just making things up for why he wasn't there just joking around. Usually when people are joking around I join in and I always try to make up the most outrageous thing I could think of and just all of a sudden what came to my mind to type was that Benoit killed his wife like the guy in Ohio did. . . ."

_JUPITER, according to the sheriff report, was traced to a Mariano Escobedo. Detective Shelton tried to call Escobedo on August 23, 2007, and received no answer at the residence. "I left a message," he wrote in his report. That was the extent of the dragnet on Escobedo.

(The number in the report was actually a cell phone in Phoenix. There was also a land-line number listed for Mariano Escobedo, at the Victorville, California, address in the report; when I called it, the person who answered, speaking in Spanish, said Mariano was a relative but did not live there. At the cell phone number in the report, I got only an incomprehensible outgoing message.)

Wrestling Observer's Meltzer, of course, had not reported that Nancy was dead, or that Chris was a murderer or anything remotely similar. Asked about Wikipedia on cable news, Meltzer instantly declared it a "nonstory." He cited the frequent gossip shorthand on discussion boards and chat rooms, "Meltzer said . . .," whenever a star wrestler missed an appearance and someone was trying to sound authoritative with a wild rumor. But in the middle of this little play to his vanity, Meltzer may not have realized that while some premature online references to Nancy's death indeed inaccurately called Meltzer the source, the Wikipedia posts were not among them. Meltzer, like the sheriff, never stopped to look into whether all Benoit rumors that day were created equal. Some could have been "non-stories" and others could have been real stories.

In the sheriff's report, a copy of the Matthew Greenberg interview was said to have been "sent to the Sheriff's Office and . . . included in the case file." (Contemporaneously, the *Stamford Advocate* had reported that the interview was on videotape, but the police there did not release Greenberg's name.) In addition, Detective Shelton wrote, the report from the search of Greenberg's computer was "attached to this supplemental."

But I found that the Greenberg interview was *not* included. And the computer report was *not* attached.

At first, sheriff's attorney Rick Lindsey explained to me that the report was wrong, that the video was never received but now was being acquired "from the law enforcement agency [Stamford police] which conducted the interview." Some time later, Lindsey changed that explanation. He said Harper told him that the task of reviewing the videotape had been delegated to another detective (presumably Shelton), who, instead of viewing it, simply discussed it with Stamford's Dolan. "To my knowledge, FCSO never had possession of the videotape. . . . [W]e don't live in a perfect world and mistakes are made. Let me see if we can get this corrected," Lindsey emailed me.

Four days after that, on July 1, 2008, came a third version. "We have had and still do have the video they sent us," Harper wrote via Lindsey, but it "cuts out after just a couple of minutes, so there is no recorded interview. I used Det. Shelton's summary for my report. Det. Shelton spoke directly to Det. Dolan and Matt Greenberg and had first-hand knowledge from both perspectives."

There is nothing quite as breathtaking as "first-hand knowledge" of secondary sources.

At my request, Fayette County sent me a copy of the partial interview in its possession, which cut off after three minutes. But the sheriff's office refused to confirm that it was requesting a complete and faithful copy from Stamford to make the open records whole.

And the Stamford cops played along. "From what I understand," Stamford Captain Richard Conklin told me, "the dupe that we made and sent down south of our video cut off for some reason after some time. But our original is ok. I think they've requested a copy." That was in Conklin's second conversation with me. In our first conversation days earlier, before he knew the missing video was about to send out a stench, Conklin had tried to imply that Greenberg was a juvenile of twelve or thirteen, rather than a nineteen-year-old young adult.

I requested a copy of the full interview directly from Stamford. In response, the police claimed an exemption under Connecticut law. I filed a complaint with the Connecticut Freedom of Information Commission, and the Stamford police capitulated and provided the video in November 2008, just before our scheduled hearing. The complete interrogation is now viewable through links on the Wrestling Babylon News blog and on YouTube.*

***

---

* My complaint to the Connecticut Freedom of Information Commission and supporting documents are included in the companion disk. See "Order the DVD" at the back of this book.

The chance that Matthew Greenberg didn't just guess, but rather had stumbled onto a sliver of inconvenient truth, cannot be rejected out of hand. Did he have an acquaintance with Chavo Guerrero, whose Wikipedia page he had cleaned up? No one asked Greenberg. Did he have a friend or relative who worked for WWE or one of its contractors? No one asked. What was the specific language of the posts that inspired his Wiki edit about Nancy Benoit dying, and on what discussion boards did he read it? The cops in WWE's home city appear to have hardly lifted a finger to find out the answers to any of these questions.

And what about the second Wikipedia edit from Australia? That didn't get a first look from Fayette County, let alone a second.*

Drilling into the discussion threads of that period on some of the most popular wrestling fan boards, I noticed that not all the archives were intact. Madison Carter, the moderator of the board at a site called WrestleCrap, told me he had "a hidden board that contains all the Benoit stuff from that night that we didn't outright delete, only accessible by my mods [moderators] and I."

Lots of hard and soft information flew around on wrestling sites that Sunday, and not all of it was reliable even when it emanated from usually reliable sources. Meltzer himself, in reporting that Chris Benoit's status

---

* That IP address, 125.63.148.173, resolved to an administrator of Unwired Australia, a wireless network offering carrier-grade Internet services. The administrator, Roger Lienert, told me, "I am responsible for the IP address ranges allocated to our company which are then allocated to our customers when they connect to the Internet. It would have been one of our customers that looked up the website you mention."

for *Vengeance* was up in the air due to a family emergency, was given incorrect information by a WWE source that Benoit had flown home from Texas. Because the report came from Meltzer, this error took on a life of its own; to this day, even many fans who closely followed the drama do not realize that Benoit was never in Texas that week but home in Georgia the whole time. This widely held misunderstanding would complicate efforts to make the proper connections, and reject the improper ones, between and among his Saturday cover story (that Nancy and Daniel had food poisoning and were throwing up blood), his Sunday text messages, and the Monday news of the three deaths.

The reporting of the food-poisoning story is a key to determining whether posts on boards Sunday night were anything but fabrication. Meltzer did not report the story prior to its publication in WWE.com's first timeline, but his memory of when he first heard it varied (in one version of his responses to my questions, Meltzer said Monday; in another, Sunday). Whether it came from Guerrero and Armstrong or from management, many wrestlers were trading that story in the dressing room in Houston as they wondered if Benoit would show up. Meltzer never clarified for his readers any details behind the dissemination of what, in retrospect, was a cover story.

Another wrestling journalist, Bob Ryder of 1wrestling .com, was the first to report the food-poisoning angle, and he did so before it became part of the first WWE timeline. At 6:36 p.m. Monday, Ryder posted a story headlined "More Details on Death of Chris Benoit & Family," which included this scoop: "Benoit had been scheduled to appear on a WWE house show on Saturday.

Sources tell us Benoit called to first say he would be taking a later flight, and then to say he would not be attending the house show due to a family illness. According to one source, Benoit said both his wife and son were throwing up blood and he needed to stay to take care of them."

There appear to be no earlier online references to the Benoits' purported bout with food poisoning. Most significantly, there are none as early as Sunday. Or, at least, none that survive.

What does it all mean? It means that not only crackpots should wonder what people at all levels of WWE knew, and when they knew it.

When a cover story collides with the discovery of the crime it is covering up, the scales fall from the beholder's eyes. The Fayette County authorities didn't care. But WWE must have cared a lot, since a thorough investigation of Greenberg's Wikipedia edit held the threat of blowing the company's timeline out of the water. For WWE, it was better not to get into all that. The sheriff obliged.

While the Wiki mischief itself may indeed have had no basis, the immediate willingness of insiders to give Matthew Greenberg a pass didn't allay suspicions. It strengthened them.

CHAPTER 10

Squire David Taylor Drops by Green Meadow Lane

AT THE SAME TIME THE Fayette County Sheriff's deputies were discovering the corpses of Daniel, Nancy, and Chris Benoit, WWE wrestler Dave Taylor and his wife, Lisa, were also, inexplicably, spotted on Green Meadow Lane. This is well established, along with Taylor's lies about it. As is the case with so much of the Benoit timeline mystery, however, it is not known who put Taylor up to this mission and what it entailed, or what, if anything, he was covering up when he lied. This chapter endeavors to make some sense out of Taylor's role.

A wrestler from Yorkshire, England, David Taylor adopted the gimmick used by a number of British performers who make it to these shores: relying on technical ability and a faux patrician air. Anyone listening carefully to his particular accent would identify it as far closer to Cockney than to Knightsbridge, but then again, we're not talking about *Masterpiece Theatre*. (On the independent wrestling circuit, he has been billed as "Squire" David Taylor.)

He and Lisa were part of Chris and Nancy's original group of WCW Peachtree City friends. In addition, Dave and Chris went all the way back to the early 1990s as tag-team partners in the German Catch Wrestling Association. With fellow Brit William Regal and the Irish Dave "Fit" Finlay, Taylor founded an Atlanta-area wrestling school called the Blue Bloods Academy. Like the others, Taylor eventually landed in WWE, first in 2000–01 and again in 2006. But unlike Benoit, Taylor never achieved main-event status or got himself "over" with a line of evolving feuds and gimmicks. In his second WWE stint, Taylor's main duties became training the young talent in Deep South Wrestling, one of the company's "developmental" territories, based in McDonough, twenty miles east of Fayetteville. In 2007 Dave and Lisa lived in Tyrone, another town in Fayette County.

The Taylors' presence near the crime scene, well before anyone in the general public could have known it might be a crime scene, is not seriously disputable. Indeed, because even the Taylors might not have realized it was a crime scene, one fork of entirely innocent speculation follows. Several sources reported seeing Lisa and an unidentified woman carrying prepared dishes of deli food, such as would be offered to console a bereaved family. This would imply that the Taylors believed one or more, but not all, of the Benoits had died, and non-violently at that — or, alternatively, it would suggest that they wished to convey as much. Even that little cannot be asserted with certitude. All we really know is that, for some reason, Dave Taylor felt the need to prevaricate rather than to explain.*

---

* Native Southerners have special protocols for food offerings to the bereaved, and one source commented to me that Lisa Taylors' dish was so

A memo by one of Mike Benoit's lawyers, Patricia Roy, has the following account:

> Holly [Schrepfer] told me early on that WWE had Dave and Lisa Taylor appear at Green Meadow house and try to get information from Holly. Holly ran into Dave and Lisa immediately after discovering the bodies, and it appeared to her that Dave and Lisa Taylor knew about what happened, though Holly thought that would be impossible because Holly was the first one to discover what happened. After speaking to Holly outside Green Meadow, Dave and Lisa Taylor would not call Holly directly and would have a mutual friend who taught horseback riding call her. Holly thought it was weird that the couple called her via the mutual friend and they thought it was weird that a week later they called and kept emphasizing to her that they did not know what had happened prior to being told by Holly and just didn't want it to appear to her that that was the case.

In the summer of 2008, I twice discussed this account with Taylor in phone conversations. Each time he denied that he was even in Georgia during that period; he claimed he was in Texas with the WWE tour crew. When the front office called him, he said, "They wanted to know where Benoit lives. They didn't even know I was in Texas, not

---

sloppily put together that it wouldn't have complied. But that analysis is a bit too inside-baseball to be useful; besides, Dave Taylor himself is not Southern and I don't know about Lisa. According to another source, the food was not purported to comfort the family after a death, but rather to give to the people in the Benoit home recovering from a bout of food poisoning. In that case, something bland, such as chicken broth, would have been more appropriate than a deli platter of complex fatty foods. Again, this is all speculation.

Georgia. I told them that, and I told them I'd never been to Benoit's house and didn't know where he lived."

Clarifying, I asked Taylor if he was saying that he was at the house show in Beaumont on Saturday, at the pay-per-view in Houston on Sunday, or at the *Raw* shoot in Corpus Christi on Monday. He said he was at all three — in Texas continuously throughout the Benoit crisis. He insisted that the first he knew of the Benoits' deaths was when Vince McMahon gathered the talent to inform them at the mid-afternoon Monday meeting in Corpus Christi.

However, sources confirmed that Taylor was not booked to wrestle in Beaumont on June 23. If he were an agent — WWE now officially calls them "producers," the backstage people who go over the finishes with the boys and keep things running smoothly — then he would have been in Houston and Corpus Christi; WWE subsidizes the presence of an expanded crew at pay-per-views and television shoots. But Taylor was not an agent; he was talent, in descent on the wrestler food chain and mostly idle except when called upon to train inexperienced wrestlers near his Georgia home.

After consulting with an insider who referred to company records, I confronted Taylor on the phone a second time, but he stuck to his guns. He maintained that he could have been in Beaumont no matter what the records showed. He said a number of non-booked wrestlers regularly travel to and hang out at WWE house shows on their own to serve as backups and to collect "draws," or cash advances on their contract guarantees. An authoritative source told me that this contention by Taylor was nonsense. While WWE overbooks pay-per-views and TV to some extent, it is not in the habit of throwing away money every night on wrestlers who don't perform.

Through every conceivable avenue, I sought contact with the Benoits' other old Peachtree City friends. The point people for this group were Penny Dunham, the widow of Johnny Grunge, and Jill Ewing, the ex-wife of a Turner Broadcasting cameraman. Eventually Ewing talked to me.

Most accounts of the estrangement between the Benoits and their neighbors present it in terms of a slow and passive withdrawal by Chris. But for Ewing, it was a bitter and specific falling-out, precipitated by the tendencies of both Chris and Nancy to try to control with whom their friends chose to associate.

"Chris was not one of my favorite people," Jill said bluntly. From there, her assessment of him zigged and zagged. She said he was great with children, and when they were first friends, in the 1990s, "I would have left my kids with him in a minute."

On the other hand, she said Chris's final text messages to Chavo Guerrero and Scott Armstrong were not strange at all, if you knew anything about him. "Chris's drug of choice was ecstasy," a synthetic stimulant/hallucinogen, Ewing said. "He did and said weird things like that all the time."

As for Dave and Lisa Taylor on Green Meadow Lane on June 25, 2007, Ewing later sent me an email in which she confirmed that Penny Dunham told her the Taylors were "looking for the house at the time the police were there. They didn't know where it was."

An Atlanta television reporter also confirmed some basics: "I was told that when investigators arrived, there were WWE wrestlers' wives already there. And yet that is not mentioned in the [sheriff's] report."

Before Mike Benoit cut off contact with me (because of

my refusal to embrace his theory that Chris's concussions supplanted, rather than supplemented, steroids as the main factor in his irrational behavior), he passed along bits and pieces of information from Holly Schrepfer. On April 26, 2008, Mike quoted her in an email: "I may have a lead for Mr. Muchnick on a few people he needs to speak with. I had a conversation with someone who was at the scene that said that things didn't look right but was uncomfortable elaborating. I have not pushed him for info yet but I will at the right time."

Detective Harper's final report said nothing at all about the Taylors. In an April 8, 2008, email to me, Harper said his own conversations with Schrepfer "did not involve anything about her speaking to the WWE that I can remember." He was responding to my question of "people from WWE talking to her almost immediately after she emerged from the crime scene, and other ongoing contacts by WWE people and intermediaries." Our dialogue ceased before I could get Harper to clarify whether he would have considered a Schrepfer-Taylor conversation to constitute "speaking to the WWE."

What the Taylors were up to is anybody's guess, but once again the lies, so free-floating and gratuitous, legitimize a round of responsible guesswork. Perhaps WWE asked Dave and Lisa to see if they could check on the Benoits on Saturday, Sunday, and/or early Monday, simply to complete the picture. As noted earlier, it is not intuitive that the pricey Andrews International security firm merely made one or two phone calls on behalf of WWE. By the same standard, it makes sense that a local on the payroll might have been utilized to supplement the effort to track down the Benoits.

Or perhaps, following the call to 911, the Taylors were

just lurking so as to learn facts the instant they emerged. In truth, the worst PR nightmare for WWE might have been a scenario in which Chris was found to have killed Nancy and Daniel but *not* himself.

Whether or not the Taylors counted among them, WWE certainly had vast organizational resources and methods at its disposal. In July 2007, according to Mike Benoit, a former Federal Bureau of Investigation special agent named Clifford E. Cormany Jr. would present his business card at the Fayette County Sheriff's Office and say he represented the family. "That was not true," Benoit told me. "We later found out he was working for WWE." A 26-year FBI veteran, Cormany had turned in his G-man badge to found in Decatur, Georgia, Investigative & Polygraph Group, Inc., "a professional association of former FBI agents" specializing in private investigations, polygraph examinations, and security consulting. (Cormany did not respond to emails, and the sheriff and WWE spokesman Davis refused to comment on him.)

What is most clear about a small fry like Dave Taylor is that he was yet another emblem of a completely closed system — a corporate culture that keeps pro wrestlers under the thumb of management while they, and they alone, bear responsibility for a range of decisions, inside and outside the ring, legal and not, monumental and petty. Benoit did the crime. Since so many drugs were found throughout the house, it doesn't appear that Taylor, or anyone else, had been charged with the task of hiding or disposing of them. Still, Taylor can be presumed to have done as he was told, whatever he was told. WWE's reward for his loyalty was to release him early in 2008.

Despite all that, Taylor may still have had his eye on the prize of a high-paying WWE gig in the future after yet another run through the indies. When in doubt, a wrestler clamps the truth in a painful submission hold, no matter how comically the fib is exposed. And even death is something to be "worked," and even homicide timelines are open season for "kayfabe."

Embedded in such whimpers, disguised as bangs, lay the ultimate secrets and lessons of the Benoit tragedy.

CHAPTER 11

How the Media Massaged It
(Tabloid, Mainstream, and Fan Flavors)

THREE MAIN STORIES WERE splashing across the celebrity coverage on cable TV news networks on June 25, 2007. Britney Spears was rumored to be dating her drug counselor. Lindsay Lohan, who had checked herself into a drug rehabilitation center after a wild Memorial Day weekend, was confirmed to be extending her stay there. And Paris Hilton was being released from a Los Angeles County jail after doing three days there on a drunk-driving rap.

In crime news, bail was set at $5 million for a former police officer in Ohio named Bobby Cutts Jr., who had murdered his pregnant girlfriend in front of their two-year-old son before rushing off to interview for the job as coach of his old high school football team.

For interludes over the next two weeks, the Chris Benoit double murder-suicide would overshadow all these stories. It combined the celebrity-mongering of the Spears-Lohan-Hilton party-girl indiscretions with the heinous crime aspects of the Cutts case. Live satellite feeds on CNN, Fox News, and MSNBC beamed news conferences and interviews with law enforcement figures, along with scenes of gawkers who had made pilgrimages to the front gate, providing eerie visuals for the haunted house in the distant background. Nancy Grace and Glenn Beck on CNN, Bill O'Reilly and Sean Hannity and Alan Colmes on Fox, and Dan Abrams on MSNBC, among others, hosted rotating panels of the same handful of journalists, current and retired wrestlers, and criminal and psychology experts to sift the known information and hazard guesses as to what had happened with the Benoits and why.

In his chapter of the book *Benoit: Wrestling with the Horror That Destroyed a Family and Crippled a Sport* (which I also co-authored), writer Steven Johnson did a quantitative analysis of both the content of the cable coverage and its impact on viewer ratings. In retrospect, the lack of staying power of that influential slice of the coverage is not at all surprising, but simply the nature of the beast. Moreover, I have concluded that the coverage itself, a fat target for derision, merited a few strangled cheers. Benoit was a sensational tabloid story, one that cable told as only cable could, with unflinching rough justice — a mess in the details, yet somewhat better overall than its critics would allow. Errors, such as Nancy Grace's repeated one about Benoit having just been "demoted from the Four Horsemen to ECW," were incidental to the larger truth that the industry had not earned the benefit of the doubt or the right to weasel out of this latest and most grisly installment of its drugs-and-death scandals.*

---

* A clique of "heel" wrestlers built around Ric Flair, the Four Horsemen were a gimmick in which Benoit had participated years earlier, when he was with World Championship Wrestling. ECW was WWE's third-tier brand. It is debatable whether Benoit's more recent shift there — albeit to a top spot

Even the *bête noire* of the tabloid coverage, all that discussion of "roid rage," wasn't as egregious as nitpickers would have it. Defenders of Benoit's image, both within his family and inside his sport, would like to deny as a factor — much less as the most important factor — that he possessed and used enough anabolics to muscle up a moose. They noted that Benoit's methodical crime spree, across an entire weekend, did not jibe with 'roid rage, which is more typically associated with short and spontaneous bursts of anger. But these apologists never conceded that clinical studies also isolate depression as a symptom of long-term steroid abuse.

Nancy Benoit likely wouldn't have been too interested in splitting these hairs: she and Daniel were just as dead regardless of what name you attached to Chris's emotional problems. Over the last months of their lives, she repeatedly exhorted Chris to clean himself up. As Nancy pointed out in her bull's-eye text message, "We both know the wellness program is a joke."

***

Cable coverage shaped public perception of the Benoit tragedy. But the mainstream media were just along for the ride. Since the story was local, the *Atlanta Journal-Constitution* and Atlanta TV stations threw resources at it. Since Benoit was Canadian and pro wrestling has more of a hold on the imaginations of legitimate sports

---

and with anticipated "player-coach" responsibilities — depressed him or triggered anxiety about the impending end of his career. Ray Rawls' memory of what Benoit said about it did not indicate that he was bothered by it. (See Chapter 5.) But it could have been a small part of the equation.

fans there, news organizations to the north also gave the story slightly longer legs. The New York tabloids, the *Daily News* and the *Post*, got in a few shots.

The *New York Times* was the first to float the theory that Benoit's many untreated concussions may have been responsible for unhinging him. The *Times* attributed the theory to former WWE wrestler Chris Nowinski, who himself had been forced to retire from the ring due to brain trauma before setting up the Sports Legacy Institute, which promotes concussion-related studies and reforms. Nowinski was a Harvard alumnus. Harvard alums have an easier time getting the ear of the *New York Times* than the rest of us.

In the run-up to possible Congressional hearings that never materialized, the *Washington Post* ran a long narrative linking the Benoit family deaths with the industry pandemic.

NBC's *Dateline* planned a Benoit documentary, then canceled it after failing to get both sides of the family on camera.

CNN's Special Investigations Unit did complete and air a November 2007 documentary called *Death Grip: Inside Pro Wrestling*. The piece had its moments, especially in exposing the WWE drug-testing loopholes, which were defended, none too convincingly, by Vince and Linda McMahon in an extended interview. But the CNN producers seemed to have paid a craven price for the McMahons' sit-down, scrubbing a counterpoint interview with industry authority Dave Meltzer.

The suspicion that banning Meltzer from the broadcast was a WWE quid pro quo cannot be proven, but that type of tactic has been evident throughout the company's media relations history. (When the Benoit toxicology reports were released, wwe representatives did live interviews on cnn's *Nancy Grace* on condition that wrestling newsletter writers Meltzer and Bryan Alvarez, who were also on the program, not appear on screen at the same time.) If it did happen that way, the blame lay with the documentary producers, who also did sloppy work in another area. cnn showed footage in which wwe's biggest star, John Cena, supposedly got caught answering with a non-denial the question of whether he had ever used steroids: "I can't tell you that I haven't, but you'll never be able to prove that I have." wwe had taped the exchange with its own hidden camera, and after the documentary was broadcast, the company posted the complete Cena interview on its website, establishing that he had been quoted outrageously out of context. He was clearly referring to a hypothetical denial of steroid use by a hypothetical someone else.

For the record, Cena himself always offers a categorical denial. Categorical but questionable. In 2007–08 he missed months of action after surgery for a torn pectoral muscle — one of those injuries that were almost never seen before the steroid era but now are found among users.

In partnership with Chris Nowinski, Mike Benoit took to the airwaves in his campaign to explain his son's multiple murders as the culmination of untreated brain damage from reckless wrestling chair shots and bumps. abc and cnn both did Benoit brain-damage exclusives in 2007, and early the next year the Sports Legacy Institute doctors reproduced their findings as part of an hour-long piece, *A Fight to the Death*, on the Canadian Broadcasting Corporation's *the fifth estate*. The concussion research got snapped up for its freshness and probably, as well, for its unconscious appeal to the sympathy of Chris's fans who, like his father, did not want to believe the worst about him. Unfortunately, the concussion theory, which had value, was grossly oversold. At best, untreated concussions are part and parcel of the same culture that bred steroid mania; concussions can supplement, but not replace, drugs as the explanation for the Benoit tragedy.

During the same period, Bennet Omalu, one of the forensic pathologists who developed the postmortem brain analysis showing unhealthy protein spots on Benoit's brain — indicating severe damage that could only be attributed to repeated hard blows to the head — authored a book, *Play Hard, Die Young: Football, Dementia, Depression and Death*. Omalu's research resonated more in the press for the anecdotes of his studies of the brains of Mike Webster, Terry Long, and Andre Waters: three National Football League players who died young, in two cases by suicide, after scary post-career trajectories of mental illness.

But despite its useful spotlight on brain injuries in every corner of sports, Dr. Omalu's book sinks under circular logic. The doctor asserts — sometimes with a degree of rationalization echoing that of the players themselves, and conflicting with the known record — that Webster, Long, and Waters were not steroid users, or at least not heavy enough users to explain the dementia syndrome. And the syndrome itself, dubbed "Chronic Traumatic Encephalopathy" or CTE, turns out to be a catch-all: vague enough to include just about anything Omalu wants, from depression, paranoia, and anxiety, to phobias and insomnia, to alcohol abuse. Omalu's methodology has major cause-and-effect flaws.

Most revoltingly, *Play Hard, Die Young*, a thin volume, does not confine itself to science. A fervent Catholic following a strain of mysticism found especially in his native Nigeria, Omalu relates the time a brain that he was transporting in his car for an autopsy started playing supernatural tricks, such as spontaneously turning on the Omalu home dishwasher in the middle of the night. Without a shred of doubt or irony, the doctor construes this as a sign from the heavens that he had a calling to get to the bottom of CTE. Which, of course, calls to mind yet another one of CTE's laundry list of purported symptoms: "increasing religiosity and quasi-spiritual insights."

***

The root flaws of the Benoit coverage were epitomized in the treatment of the Wikipedia affair by the Associated Press, the wire service collective that is subscribed to by many mainstream news outlets of all sizes. For several days from late June through early July 2007, thousands of newspapers, radio and television stations, and websites hyped, then summarily declared a nonstory, the mystery of why an unauthorized Wikipedia editor had posted the news that Nancy Benoit was dead before that fact was publicly known (see Chapter 9). These secondary accounts had many different bylines, and they cut-and-pasted different facts and emphases from the AP stories, as rewrites of wire copy always do. But all the stories jumped to the same faulty conclusion, based at least in part on the same erroneous fact.

According to the LexisNexis database, the first AP file on Benoit and Wikipedia came through on June 28 at

9:57 p.m., Greenwich mean time. Subsequent feeds over the next forty-eight hours never wavered on one key paragraph:

> WWE attorney Jerry McDevitt said that to his knowledge, no one at the WWE knew Nancy Benoit was dead before her body was found Monday afternoon. Text messages released by officials show that messages from Chris Benoit's cell phone were being sent to co-workers a few hours after the Wikipedia posting.

The second sentence is false: Benoit's text messages were sent nearly twenty-four hours *before* the Wikipedia edit. Further, WWE itself had published the chronology of those messages two days earlier. So how did AP get duped?

I put the question to Harry Weber, the AP reporter who wrote the above paragraph. Was McDevitt the source for the statement that the Wikipedia edit preceded the text messages?

Weber said in an email, "To be clearer, the story should have said the messages were 'received' by various people after the Wikipedia posting, rather than were 'sent' after the posting. At that early stage in the case, there was confusion caused by police, WWE attorney and others as to the timeline." Weber acknowledged that AP spoke to McDevitt "at length."

I followed up: "Since you were aware that the sending of the texts preceded the Wikipedia edit, is there a reason why the story didn't explain that?" I added that I was trying to figure out if the confusion was deliberately sown. (Tactfully, I failed to add that the text messages were already in both versions of the WWE timeline.)

Weber: "I do believe some of the confusion caused by the timeline discrepancies provided by the WWE were [*sic*] intentional. We used a lot of discretion and news judgment and the best information available at the time."

A few days later Weber backed away from an earlier promise to talk further with me. "AP does not allow reporters to comment outside of AP or discuss our stories beyond what we have reported. I must exercise caution and not proceed any further. I think you are on the right track in the line of inquiry you are pursuing," he said.

AP also perpetuated an inaccurate statement by McDevitt, in its June 27 stories, about the sources of all the steroids found in Benoit's home:

> Long-time WWE attorney (and former personal attorney of Hulk Hogan) Jerry McDevitt said all of the steroids found in Benoit's home were from a legitimate prescription. "We know which doctor prescribed it," he said. "There's no question, none of these drugs are out there, none of these drugs came from Internet pharmacies."

In fact, one of the first sets of drugs, if not the very first, found by detectives was a refrigerated stash of growth hormone with the label of a Chinese company. McDevitt surely intended to refer to the Dr. Astin prescriptions filled by several local pharmacies. But the Chinese growth hormone likely came from an Internet purveyor, such as Signature Pharmacy. (Chapter 12 treats this subject in depth.)

No one is perfect; errors of all sizes and shapes litter coverage of all subjects. But what the Benoit story showed was how easily, in a downscale subject like wrestling, one or two planted misstatements, nudging the narrative toward closure, can turn off the spigot. In scandals, it is often the drip-drip-drip of accumulated detail that wears down the limestone wall. Here we had more like a splash, followed by a towel-down.

***

As with all coverage by the wrestling fan media, the Benoit story was driven by Dave Meltzer's *Wrestling Observer*, the granddaddy of the "kayfabe sheets," dating back to the 1970s, and the largest and most influential publication of its kind. Though Meltzer does not release circulation figures, the *Observer*'s weekly print edition is believed to have thousands of readers. Many more thousands browse the free and premium versions of its website. In 1990–91, Meltzer wrote a column on pro wrestling for *The National*, a short-lived daily sports newspaper. Later in the decade he reported from the ground floor on the nascent sport of mixed martial arts; like boxing, MMA is not choreographed, but to some extent shares with wrestling a type of athletic talent and promotional infrastructures and methods. After stints covering MMA for the *Los Angeles Times* and FoxSports .com, Meltzer is now a prolific MMA columnist for Yahoo Sports — this in addition to churning out, basically by himself, more than 30,000 words a week, fifty-two weeks a year, for the hard copy and electronic versions of the *Observer*.

Meltzer's astonishing output is the apex of a quasi-journalistic genre in diverse media, which has attracted passionate above- and underground followings. In the

1980s the market dominance of the then–World Wrestling Federation, which had begun publishing a captive line of slick newsstand magazines, ended the heyday of old-school independent pulp wrestling mags. The best known of these were *Pro Wrestling Illustrated* and its sister titles, published by Stanley Weston and edited by Bill Apter. *PWI* lingers in new incarnations, but little else from that category survives.

The wrestling magazines, at least as originally conceived, were analogous to Hollywood fan fluff, with apocryphal reporting that pushed favored stars and obeyed the industry's internal practice of suspending disbelief even to the extent of not divulging that wrestling was staged. Meltzer's *Observer* — launched in his youth, sustained as a hobby while he held down conventional newspaper sports writing jobs immediately after college, and eventually developed into a lucrative full-time business and mini-empire — irrevocably changed the rules of wrestling journalism in its refusal to perpetuate that particular illusion. Like the "Apter mags" (as the new breed of so-called "smart" fans now remember them), Meltzer covered the theatrical product presented in arenas and on television screens. But Meltzer added a layer of authentic behind-the-scenes reporting and analysis. He was a genuine industry expert who brought to more discerning readers the real stories of backstage politics and the real data about wrestling's contracts, booking decisions, conflicts, growth, and emerging profile in the sports and entertainment worlds.

As wrestling's Mafia-like territorial system collapsed — to be replaced by the global hegemony of McMahon's marketing-driven WWF/WWE — Meltzer also demonstrated, among other crossover skills, an extraordinary flair for

183

in-depth quick-scan interpretation of things like television ratings and corporate securities disclosure statements. Generally speaking, no one could quantify better than Dave Meltzer. His wrestler death list, compiled during the Benoit frenzy, was the best around; unlike fellow empiricists such as *USA Today*, Meltzer knew the difference between a wrestler who OD'd and, say, the right-on-schedule fatal heart attack of Andre the Giant, who had a medical condition that made him freakishly large and handed to him, on the same platter, both a lucrative wrestling career and a ticket to an early demise.

In the same vein, Meltzer refused to pander to fans who jumped on the Benoit concussion bandwagon, but neither did he whitewash that factor. The *Observer* listed 62 "major league" wrestling deaths in the decade up through Benoit's career, and Meltzer broke them down. "ECW [the original Philadelphia-based "hard-core" trailblazer, Extreme Championship Wrestling] definitely was the worst of the three majors [also including WWF/WWE and Ted Turner's World Championship Wrestling] in terms of deaths per capita, probably because it had the worst drug issues and the hard-head-trauma style," Meltzer said. "But if you look at all the deaths, the vast majority took no more head trauma than wrestlers of any other generation who didn't have the death rate. Drugs, whether painkillers or steroids, and probably the combination of them, to me is a much stronger factor when you look at the individual cases. Everyone wants an easy answer, and it's no different with those who jumped on the steroid bandwagon."

He summed up: "Concussions were no factor with Eddie Guerrero, for example, or with Davey Boy Smith [who also suffered a fatal heart attack, in 2002]. It's very possible they played a part with Chris, but how can you dismiss other things that lead to depression when it was a crime of depression?"

Educated by analysis such as this, "smart" fans multiplied on the World Wide Web, creating dozens upon dozens of fan news sites (many, though not all, cribbing content from Meltzer), discussion boards, chat rooms, and other communication and social-networking tools. Today a few other regular print newsletters thrive alongside the *Observer,* the most prominent being Wade Keller's *Pro Wrestling Torch* and Bryan Alvarez's *Figure Four Weekly* (the latter is an online affiliate of the *Observer*).

In the quarter-century of my own relationship with Meltzer, I have found him an indefatigably helpful resource. Even though our perspectives often differ, he has never been too busy to review a draft of an article or a chapter, or to answer even the most seemingly trivial factual question. I appreciate that quality and deeply respect his original body of work, which deserves more credit than anything else for imbuing its offbeat subject with a reasonably accurate history and literature. Quirky and intrinsically fascinating, the *Wrestling Observer* is a model of entrepreneurism.

The decision to build this book around the timeline mystery was largely shaped by facts and insights Meltzer conveyed to me but not to his readership at large. This would both enrich my research and become a source of tension between us. When we discussed the centrality to my theme of WWE's "worked" *Raw* tribute to Benoit, Dave said in an email, "It's an angle I'd push pretty hard." He added, apparently half-facetiously, "Can I write it?"

Cynically conditioned to dismiss WWE's manipulations of public opinion as matters of taste only, without larger lessons for its culture of death, I might never have zeroed in on the *Raw* nugget if not for Meltzer's encouragement. He corroborated company executives' earlier-than-acknowledged information pointing to murder-suicide — a 6:05 eastern time call to him from a well-placed Canadian source, which aligned with what a Royal Canadian Mounted Police report documented and Mike Benoit had already verified (see Chapter 6). For me, Meltzer's corroboration then became the impetus for "reverse-engineering" the company's overall shaky timeline subsequent to Chris's criminal acts. Since Benoit was unquestionably the perpetrator of the murders, exploring that shaky timeline and its meaning became this book's investigative mission.

But as research proceeded from there, Dave and I did not see eye-to-eye on my approach, and I told him so and he told me so. I thought the *Observer* published far too little about the case, and without nearly enough persistence, to the point where, wittingly or not, Meltzer enabled the resumption of business as usual. While I don't presume to put words in his mouth, he clearly disliked the style of much of my blog reporting and writing, and felt I alienated potentially helpful long-term sources.

That was where the rubber hit the road. For all its ridicule of the mainstream media's shallow grasp of wrestling, the *Observer* and the other sheets themselves operate like gossip networks. At a certain point — a very early one, considering the amount of muck raked — they circle the wagons around the people in the industry they cover. Meltzer bore the brunt of my exhortations to the wrestling journalism community to do a better job of exposing the essence of the Benoit saga so as to spur overdue reforms in drug testing and talent management. Dave didn't always take kindly to the suggestion that he might be part of the problem rather than the solution; like insiders in Washington politics or anything else, he tends to exaggerate in his own mind what he risks and to downplay how much he protects. His paternalistic modus operandi demands a set of assumptions I don't share.

Over time, I had to confront the implications of what Meltzer chose to say and not say, for they added up to an unresolved paradox. Tipped almost as soon as the bodies were discovered, Meltzer himself knew from day one, hour one, that WWE's *Raw* tribute was manipulative. Most of the talent on the show didn't yet realize it, but company brass already understood that they were honoring a murderer and that the news might even reach the public before *Raw*'s first feed, to the eastern two-thirds of the country, went off the air. Yet, over the next days, while cable TV news people were hammering WWE over this possibility, based only on the sort of generalized innuendo of sleaze that is routinely leveled at wrestling promoters, Dave limited himself to agreeing that WWE and the USA network might have exercised better judgment by pulling the later West Coast repeat of *Raw*.

On his website on June 26, previewing that night's SmackDown/ECW TV shoot in San Antonio, Meltzer focused on McMahon's purported sterling leadership of the troops:

> The lack of an understandable explanation to the circumstances of the death of Chris, Nancy and Daniel Benoit has left virtually the entire wrestling community reeling.

> Within WWE, the obvious questions and lack of answers are no different from fans and most of his long-time friends.

187

> Vince McMahon was the inspiring general both to the
> wrestlers as well as the office staff all day yesterday. He held
> it together and was a rock of strength for much of the talent,
> which because of their admiration and in many cases love for
> Benoit, were saddened, perplexed and having an incredibly
> difficult time dealing with it.

Eventually Meltzer told *Observer* print readers that the McMahon family "had to know" the perpetrator and nature of the crime when they green-lighted the *Raw* tribute. Instead of saying so prominently and clearly, however, Meltzer buried it in the middle of his weekly mountain of verbiage. All the while, he was urging me to push "pretty hard" my own investigation of what had happened behind the scenes at *Raw!*

Meltzer's audience admires his comprehensiveness and so do I. But in this instance and in my opinion, he generated only gobbledygook. In November 1997, when McMahon pulled strings with agents, a referee, and other wrestlers to conspire against Bret Hart, the outgoing WWF champion who was moving to rival promotion WCW, Meltzer had written the definitive account of the incident forever after known as the "Montreal screwjob." But Meltzer attempted no similar takeout on WWE's Benoit timelines. The contrast added up to a posture that the treacheries of pro wrestling choreography were more important than the full story of three brutal deaths. Never, to my knowledge, did Meltzer even cite the report about the Mounties and Mike Benoit's recollection of how he got the news — which was on my blog after being not only inspired by Meltzer, but in certain areas virtually ventriloquized by him.

Moving backwards in time from that key finding, I

went on to feed Dave voluminous details of how the Georgia authorities played fast and loose with the investigative record to stymie information on what WWE knew and when. Dave sometimes misattributed the few piecemeal stories he chose to write based on that material, stating that they resulted from new public document releases rather than from the original reporting of another writer. In and of itself, that was just a vanity issue. But Meltzer, in my view, also reported the information selectively and out of context, wrong-headedly dismissing its significance.

The missing telephonic evidence, he wrote in the newsletter, "doesn't prove anything." Yet during the same period, he was telling me privately, "One person who saw the [text message] list told me it was weird how they had some texts he sent but not several others." Meltzer's failure to investigate the timeline, or even to disclose in good faith what he knew about the validity of another reporter's investigation of the timeline, betrayed a fundamental misunderstanding of the journalistic process.

Through it all, he continued to answer my questions, to preview a couple of my blog articles on his site, and to provide other indispensable support. So what we had here was a months-long clinic in the vagaries of "wrestling communication."

It finally reached the point where I had to ask Meltzer directly why he had withheld or muted baseline information on the Benoit weekend: that the *Raw* tribute was contrived and, furthermore, a substantive opening on a host of WWE timeline discrepancies. I pointed out that in his published coverage, he had laboriously analyzed the on-camera behavior of everyone at the Corpus Christi shoot, and specifically noted the odd words and body language of Chavo Guerrero and William Regal. Most puzzlingly, Meltzer gave Vince McMahon credit for holding the crew together through that day's trauma. There was a basic disconnect between saying these things, no matter how correct each fact was in isolation, and not telling the rest of the story — that McMahon knew the score and was controlling the form and timing of how the Benoit news reached the public.

Meltzer explained to me that while the timeline was "a" story, "to me the big story was what caused Benoit to do what he did, and when it came out he was using the drugs everyone would have expected, an analysis of the ways to make the drug testing policy more honest and effective."

That explanation is unsatisfactory. Meltzer knows at least as well as anyone that an effective reporter cannot arbitrarily dictate the parameters of a story. WWE's suspicious timeline was the linchpin of the Benoit scandal at the fleeting moment when it had the public's full attention. Since how that resolved would impact the company's credibility, it was arguably the single most important factor in determining whether meaningful scrutiny of drug testing and other questionable practices of the wrestling industry would get any traction.

One of Meltzer's most-quoted observations is that if athletes in legitimate sports died at anywhere close to the rate in wrestling, the phenomenon would be front-page news. That observation seems ironic following a review of the Benoit coverage by him and other wrestling journalists. When the chips were down, they were less proactive about spurring awareness than they would like us — and themselves — to believe. Starting the day by pontificating on the uniqueness of the business, they ended it by encapsulating the question of whether the term "wrestling journalism" is an oxymoron. Quick to note the mostly trivial mistakes in non-expert renderings of biographies and urban legends, and eager to demonstrate their superior grasp of the cat-and-mouse processes of drug testing, they also behaved an awful lot like the mainstream media they criticized.

Wrestling *journalists*, after all, are wrestling *fans*; and fans have short attention spans. Fans wanted to move on from Chris and Nancy and Daniel Benoit as soon as possible, and they did . . . to Chris Jericho and Shawn Michaels' comebacks . . . to Ric Flair's retirement . . . to John Cena and Rey Mysterio's injuries and Stephanie and Triple H's family political machinations. After wiping away a tear or two, fans weren't about to interrupt their junk entertainment. Nor were the sheets that catered to them about to squander ethical capital trying to persuade them to do otherwise.

CHAPTER 12

Dr. Astin and the War on Drugs

FOR ALL WE KNOW, A POLITE RAP of knuckles on the door of Dr. Phillippe C. Astin III's office in Carrollton, Georgia, would have served just as well. But the operatives of the Atlanta office of the federal Drug Enforcement Administration not only were armed with a subpoena; they were backed up by TV cameras alerted to capture a battery of agents with the letters "DEA" on the back of their government-issue jackets. With that many beasts needing that much red meat, no simple knock on the door would suffice. Instead, viewers of CNN were treated to video of a battering ram knocking the door down. The footage looped over and over, like that Pentagon video of the bomb that had succeeded in obliterating its target in Iraq with no civilian casualties.

It was June 29, 2007 — the same day the Connecticut cops interrogated poor Matthew Greenberg — and the meter on Fayette County District Attorney Scott Ballard's fifteen minutes of fame was ticking toward zero. This was the second raid in three days on the office of Dr. Astin, who was Chris Benoit's personal physician and well known throughout the Atlanta-area sports and wrestling communities for being an easy touch with requests for prescriptions. This had put Dr. Astin in the crosshairs of the DEA and the U.S. attorney. After the Benoit family's bodies were found, indices of the flow of drugs in the region, maintained by the DEA's Office of Diversion Control, lined up with prescription information at the crime scene identifying Astin as the supplier of much of Chris's injectable testosterone and other pharmaceuticals. In a three-year period through May 9, 2007, Astin prescribed Benoit, on average, a ten-month supply of steroids every three to four weeks.

In the raids of Astin's office, agents seized copies of prescriptions "for Testosterone, Xanax, Adderall, Concerta, Hydrocodone, Oxycodone, and Soma," according to a seven-count indictment on July 2, "which were consistent, in terms of quantities, dosages, and frequencies of the prescriptions, with illegal prescription drug abuse. Multiple undated copies of prescriptions for controlled substances were also found in various medical records." The indictment documented the doctor's high volumes of prescriptions to patients "M.J." and "O.G." Though they wouldn't confirm it, the wrestling community matched up these initials with the wrestlers Mark Jindrak and Oscar Gutiérrez ("Rey Mysterio").

The public insertion of the Astin prosecution into the Benoit story meant two things. First, the family medical records, which were pertinent to the murder-suicide, remained under seal, layering puzzlement atop conundrum. Second, Scooter Ballard's rambling commentary on the varieties of the bizarre lost its dominance of the daily drumbeat of sound bites. After all, this was now, literally, a federal case.

Prosecutors also leaked other information joining

Benoit's fall to the region's drug-besotted wrestling scene. The year before, when Benoit's close friend Johnny Grunge died, empty bottles were found next to him with labels indicating they very recently contained a total of 120 Soma pills prescribed by Astin. Of course, Astin hadn't advised Dunham to take them all at once. In May 2008, federal prosecutors would issue a "superseding" indictment of Astin, adding 175 counts and several more coded wrestling names: "C.M.B." for Christopher Michael Benoit, "N.E.B." for Nancy Elizabeth Benoit, "R.W.H." for Robert William "Hardcore Holly" Howard, and "M.A.B." for Marcus Alexander "Buff" Bagwell.

On January 29, 2009, Dr. Astin pleaded guilty to all 175 counts. His attorney, Natasha Perdew Silas, explained to the judge that he was just a country doctor who "in chronic pain cases, . . . more often than not, would simply accede to the patient's request that they needed strong or stronger medicine to handle their pain." As the years went by, the lawyer said, "Dr. Astin became more and more willing to bend the rules."

***

The Astin indictment did not include counts on steroids, the congenial access to which was the doctor's most substantial claim to infamy. Technically, he was busted only for the painkillers, muscle relaxers, and sedatives heavily used by the same jocks who also abused steroids. According to law enforcement insiders, this omission reflected the embryonic state of the government's war on steroids, which escalated after President Bush pushed it in his 2004 State of the Union speech. The authorities' longer history of battling heroin, cocaine, ecstasy, and other hard-core street drugs makes possible a more direct chain of arrests for those substances. But in the early years of moving up any new distribution chain, the prosecutors must strategically go after smaller-scale users and dealers for whatever they can find in order to get them off the streets and out of business, while preserving evidence of the mass marketing of the primary targeted drug for more ambitious cases down the road against bigger fish.

The Astin prosecution revealed other steps in the evolution of anabolic enhancement and its embrace by the mainstream for both athletic and quasi-athletic purposes. These factors had informed the drug culture of pro wrestling for decades prior to reaching public consciousness.

As many sports fans now understand, the original battleground of steroids was the Olympic Games, especially in weightlifting and certain track-and-field events. It was a time when Eastern bloc countries were a step ahead of the U.S. in the technology of cheating and the Games were a major Cold War platform. By the 1960s steroids had spread to pro football, as well as to less legitimate sports like bodybuilding and pro wrestling, where the premium was on appearance more than on conventional definitions of athletic "performance." In Southern California, Venice's Muscle Beach scene was enabled by a network of gay doctors who traded illicit drugs for sexual favors and mirrored the hustling strategies of its core denizens. These were the precursors of what wrestling people would tab as "mark" doctors. Not all the doctors who effectively doubled as drug connections qualified as starry-eyed fans; but, for a price, all were willing to provide virtual blank-check scripts for steroids, as well as for the painkillers and other self-medications used to make the starving-artist lifestyle more palatable.

For wrestlers, the new drug regime had even more sinister implications than for bodybuilders, who perceived immediately how the ante had been upped and the competition skewed. Comprehension of the commercial benefits of steroids was a bit slower in wrestling, but over time, the marketplace spoke loudly and clearly there, too. With their far-flung tours and few days off, wrestlers competing for top spots on the basis of a favored artificial look did not have the opportunities of bodybuilders or seasonal athletes to use, taper, abstain, and start all over — the process known in the muscle gyms as "cycling." And every element of their punishing working conditions and the cocktails they utilized to master them reinforced and exacerbated the problem. Steroids not only built muscle mass; they also hastened recovery from hard workouts, which often were squeezed in between wrestling bookings at either end of plane or automobile trips. Synthetic derivatives of testosterone, the male hormone, seemed an obvious solution to a multitude of problems. As it turned out, though, the muscle growth from anabolic steroids also overloaded the tendons connecting muscle groups. This, in turn, caused exotic new injuries, most notably torn triceps (upper arm) and pectorals (chest). That was without even accounting for other unintended effects, which ranged from the cosmetic (back acne, swollen skulls, "bitch tits") to the alarming (shrunken testicles and impotence, liver and kidney damage, arterial blockage).

Dick "The Bruiser" Afflis, a former National Football League journeyman who hit it big in wrestling in the late 1950s, was surely one of the earliest steroid guys. Inside

197

and outside the ring, from coast to coast, the Bruiser brawled his way to main events and media attention. Wayne Coleman, a charismatic and flamboyant muscle man (and, unlike the Bruiser, a better talker than performer), became a prototype 1970s heel, "Superstar Billy Graham," and a champion of Vince McMahon's father's World Wide Wrestling Federation. Graham's gimmick inspired many other careers, including those of Jesse "The Body" Ventura, the future governor of Minnesota, and Hulk Hogan, whose style and success during the continental promotional war of the early cable TV era transformed forever pro wrestling and the expectations of its talent.

Vince McMahon was the promoter who won the war, largely through guiding Hogan to crossover stardom in the period leading up to the first *WrestleMania* in 1985. By then, 'roids were defining not just *a* look in wrestling but *the* look up and down the rosters of even less formidable promotions. The problem was made more intractable by the personal fetish for size and cartoonish muscularity of McMahon himself, who lifted weights and was "on the juice." (At the time he didn't perform, except as a TV announcer.) The fact that wrestling is "worked" put promoters in a unique position to set standards, even if it is not fully appreciated that they hardly have absolute "power of the pencil" and are destined to fail if they don't heed fan feedback. From his position as the head of the first multinational wrestling corporation, which morphed into a merchandising powerhouse, McMahon had a particular vision of maxing out on multiple revenue streams in every conceivable entertainment avenue, and it worked. His decisions on which performers to push reflected this bias. In turn, wwf's impossible-to-misinterpret signal got internalized by every independent wrestling troupe, every up-and-comer, every wannabe.

To say, as many do, that wrestlers are role models for the kids watching them on TV reduces a complex dynamic to a Parents Television Council slogan, and in so doing, vastly understates the problem. Willingness to do steroids, and just about whatever it takes in order to get oneself "over," has become as integral to wrestling's rewards system as facelifts and breast augmentation surgery are to Hollywood's.

In the years prior to Vincent Kennedy McMahon's 1982 purchase of the Northeast wrestling territory from a group headed by his father, Vincent James McMahon, and in the first two years of wwf's ambitious expansion, the promotion's syndicated television shows were taped in Allentown and Hamburg, Pennsylvania. The state athletic commission-appointed attending physician for those shows, a Harrisburg urologist and osteopath named George Zahorian, reveled in his access to the wrestlers and in his bonanza as their connection. Before Allentown shows in the '80s, wwfers lining up for their Zahorian-administered blood-pressure tests clutched hundred-dollar bills, for which the doctor swapped his bags of goodies. Zahorian also FedExed them to wrestling people — Hogan and McMahon among them — more or less on demand.

In 1990, following an undercover investigation conducted through Bill Dunn, a power-lifter and University of Virginia strength and conditioning coach, DEA agents raided Zahorian's office and arrested him. (Dunn himself faced a long list of charges before turning state's evidence, and died shortly thereafter.) The following summer, a jury found Zahorian guilty of eleven felony counts of illegally distributing controlled substances. It was the first conviction of a physician under the Anti-Drug Abuse Act of 1988, the first statute to define steroids as a controlled substance and to ban their prescription for non-therapeutic purposes. Zahorian did federal prison time in addition to paying a fine and seeing the government seize his condo office complex.

The wrestlers testifying at Zahorian's trial included Superstar Billy Graham (by now crippled by bone and joint degeneration from his decades of steroid abuse), Rowdy Roddy Piper, Rick Martel, Brian Blair, and Danny Spivey. In one of his earliest and most important interventions, lawyer Jerry McDevitt got the judge to quash Hulk Hogan's subpoena to testify. But Zahorian's shipments of steroids to Hogan still came out in court, and news accounts carried a photo of the two posing together. The scandal unraveled when Hogan went on Arsenio Hall's TV talk show, where he was expected to own up to a mistake but instead lied through his teeth, insisting he had never used steroids except on two occasions, under Zahorian's supervision, to treat injuries. Former wrestling colleagues went on the record and persuasively contradicted Hogan. And the drug scandal fueled a sex scandal when ex-WWFers came forward with anecdotes of both hetero- and homosexual harassment by company executives.

In 1994, Vince McMahon himself was in the dock in a federal courtroom on Long Island for alleged conspiracy to distribute steroids. But this time the government's case overreached: a conspiracy, by definition, requires the participation of more than one person, and the mere suggestion that WWF's booking priorities rewarded the unnaturally musclebound was insufficient to establish one. McMahon also may have lucked out. In 1990, through social connections, he had gotten a tip that Zahorian was hot, which motivated WWF to stop hiring him as a ringside doctor. During much of the period in question, Zahorian was employed by the Pennsylvania State Athletic Commission; after the passage of deregulatory legislation, there was still a requirement for a ringside physician, who henceforth would be appointed by the promotion. At McMahon's trial, the former WWF employee in charge of that task, Anita Scales, testified that she had tried to cut off Zahorian, but McMahon assistant Pat Patterson overruled her, saying, "The boys need their candy."

At McMahon's trial, McDevitt co-counseled with celebrated defense attorney Laura Brevetti (who reportedly had been on President Clinton's short list when he was seeking a woman for attorney general). Months after the not-guilty verdict at McMahon's trial, New York's *Village Voice* exposed the extracurricular razzle-dazzle of Brevetti's husband, Martin Bergman, a vaguely employed television producer and purported "fixer." Bergman had introduced himself to one of the government's star witnesses, Emily Feinberg, a former *Playboy* model. Feinberg had been McMahon's secretary and had one of his many liaisons with the hired help. In the process, the *Voice* reported, Bergman secured advance knowledge of the details of Feinberg's testimony, and the defense team was equipped for more effective cross-examination.*

The period of the trial was the ebb of WWF fortunes.

---

* Bergman was the brother of the far better-known *60 Minutes* investigative producer, Lowell Bergman, who would be portrayed by Al Pacino in *The Insider*, the movie account of corruption in the tobacco industry.

In 1998, after a several-year-long slump, the company rebounded. Indeed, driven by a new star, Steve Austin, and then by The Rock (now movie star Dwayne Johnson), WWF live attendance, TV ratings, pay-per-view subscriptions, and merchandise sales reached levels unseen even in the Hogan days. Once and for all, McMahon shook off the threat of Time Warner's Turner Broadcasting (whose mismanaged WCW would go into a shockingly rapid descent and, in 2001, close its doors). Going with the flow like any smart booker, but taking the principle to extremes, McMahon had turned himself into his own troupe's leading TV heel.

In the fall of 1999, WWF went public on the NASDAQ stock exchange, making McMahon an instant near-billionaire on paper. During the swirl of hype before the initial stock offering, he found it advantageous to put out the story not only that the federal government had persecuted him five years earlier, but also that he had been *convicted* on one of the counts of conspiracy to distribute steroids. This gave his persona a little more swagger, or something; that it happened to be untrue was . . . just wrestling. Why McMahon felt it fit the profile of an imminent Wall Street tycoon was yet another exhibit of his inside-outlaw path to fame and fortune.*

---

* World Wrestling Federation Entertainment (WWFE) — shortened to World Wrestling Entertainment (WWE) as the resolution of a trademark dispute with the World Wildlife Fund — would migrate to the New York Stock Exchange, and as initial stock prices dropped to a more realistic plateau, McMahon lost his brief residency on the Forbes 400 list of the wealthiest Americans. Still, his worth settled in the high hundreds of millions of dollars, his company had capitalization of a billion-plus, and thanks to the designations of different classes of stock, the McMahon family remained firmly in control of the company.

***

After Zahorian, the best-known mark doctor in the 1990s was Joel Hackett of Indianapolis, known among WWF wrestlers as "Dr. Feelgood." Hackett supported the addictions of Brian Pillman, who jumped to WWF from WCW in the midst of extremely eccentric behavior, most of it contrived, which earned him the nickname "the Loose Cannon." Pillman liked to joke, "I've got to get back to my hotel room and call my doctor 'cause I just can't 'hack-ett' any more." When he died, empty containers of painkillers with Hackett's name on the prescription labels lay next to Pillman.

Four months later, in February 1998, another WWF wrestler, twenty-seven-year-old Louis Mucciolo ("Louie Spicolli," a stage name inspired by Sean Penn's character in *Fast Times at Ridgemont High*), mixing alcohol with huge quantities of Soma, died in a pool of his own vomit. Alongside were an empty vial of testosterone and a Hackett-prescribed supply of Xanax.

Other prominent Hackett "patients" included Jim Hellwig ("The Ultimate Warrior"), Tony Norris ("Ahmed Johnson" in WWF, "Big T" in WCW), and Del Wilkes ("The Patriot"). The latter, one of Hackett's distributors among the boys, was arrested 20 times for forging prescriptions and in 2002 served a nine-month prison sentence.

More so than Zahorian — a poster child for steroid-pushing even though he also had a broader prescription palette — Hackett symbolized the overall lifestyle issues associated with wrestling. The same doctors who pre-scribed anabolic enhancers, with or without a sincere interest in the well-being of their patients, also processed bottomless demands for painkillers, sleeping pills, antidepressants, the whole nine yards. On the road, wrestlers swapped pharmaceuticals as freely as they did the anecdotes of their compound effects, mixing and matching whatever felt good and did the trick of getting them through interminable one-night stands.

Marc Mero was "Johnny B. Badd" in wcw and "Wildman Marc Mero" in wwe. "There is no off-season in wrestling — and I mean *no off-season*," said Mero, who wrestled Benoit in wcw. Mero now owns a gym near Orlando and runs a program spreading anti-drug messages to high schoolers. "You would do *WrestleMania*, the biggest show of the year, on a Sunday night, then turn right around and do the *Raw* shoot on Monday to set up the next batch of issues and feuds. That's the equivalent of playing the Super Bowl one day and the first game of the next football season the very next day."

Mero said Benoit was not unique in his easy access to drugs of all kinds: "You name it, you could get it. There was always a doctor hanging around, or another wrestler who knew a doctor who could cover you with a script." In tv interviews during the Benoit media frenzy and in his anti-drug lectures, Mero held up ever-growing lists of the dozens of his direct wrestling colleagues who had died young. He said no other occupation, not even military service in Iraq, could make such a dubious boast. (Mero didn't shrug off Benoit's concussions, either. He said, "I personally had matches where I didn't even remember how I got through them.")*

---

* Mero's ex-wife Rena (now married to mixed martial arts star Brock Lesnar) was "Sable," the first of the wwf divas to pose for the cover of *Playboy*.

Mindful of the Zahorian nightmare, WWF took no chances with Hackett, who would try to get to the wrestlers at events in Indiana but was barred from the dressing rooms. After Muccioli's death, the company actively fed the regional DEA office information on Hackett's shady practices. In 1999, when the Indiana Medical Board suspended Hackett's license, WWF issued a press release lauding the action and pointing out that the state attorney general's complaint "did not name any performers connected with the WWF." (The complaint did cite Hackett for illegally prescribing drugs "to at least 11 professional wrestlers.") In 2001 the feds busted Hackett on twenty-four counts of making false statements and prescriptions, and twenty-four additional counts of controlled substance fraud and deceit.

***

Chris Benoit's growth hormone from China's Gene-Science Pharmaceutical Co. Ltd. put him at the cutting edge — or maybe just the mainstream — of another phenomenon: the gray market in steroids sold across national boundaries via the Internet.

Four months after the murder-suicide, the DEA coor - dinated an international investigation, code-named "Operation Raw Deal," a series of raids on the under- ground 'roid network that marked the largest crackdown to date. With the assistance of other American agencies and their counterparts in Canada, Mexico, China, Belgium, Australia, Germany, Denmark, Sweden, and Thailand, 124 arrests and seizures were made at fifty-six labs across the U.S. The scorecard on seized items includ- ed seventy-one weapons, twenty-seven pill presses, twenty-five vehicles, and three boats. The total stockpile of 11.4 million doses of steroids (based on 0.5 milliliter per dose) amounted to 570,000 ten-milliliter vials, with a street value exceeding $50 million. That was not even including Human Growth Hormone, Insulin Growth Factor, cocaine, marijuana, ecstasy, painkillers, anti-anxiety medications, or, of course, Viagra. Federal agents told Josh Peter of Yahoo Sports that China, where more than thirty-five drug wholesalers flourished, had emerged as the leading supplier of illicit steroids and HGH since the DEA began targeting Mexican suppliers in 2005. Chinese companies stepped immediately into the breach and kept the traffic flowing.*

Domestically, the highest-profile prosecutions busted putative "pharmacies" in Florida. The geography was a clue to how the marketing of designer anabolics had simultaneously and shrewdly melded three constituencies: elite athletes, wannabes at every level — and everyone in the whole wide world after the same thing Ponce de Leon once sought. That steroids were not really fountains of youth did not matter to either the sellers or the buyers. As Billy Crystal's Fernando used to say on *Saturday Night Live*, it is more important to *look* marvelous than to *feel* marvelous.

In February 2007, fourteen people running seven Internet drug dealers out of Florida were indicted by a federal grand jury on charges of selling drugs to clients without their having visited a doctor. Prosecutors operating out of the district attorney's office in Albany, New

---

* Yahoo Sports enterprise reporter Peter's excellent coverage of Operation Raw Deal is at http://sports.yahoo.com/top/news?slug=josteroids092407 &prov=yhoo&type=lgns.

York, arrested fifteen others on similar charges, and with the additional intriguing detail that many of the virtual patients were well-known professional athletes. The ring-leader was the Orlando-based Signature Pharmacy, accused of selling $40 million worth of drugs in 2006. The leading associated sources of customers for Signature were the Palm Beach Rejuvenation Center and the website for the supplement marketer MedXlife. Signature's owners, Greg Trotta and Brian Schafler, generated phony prescriptions through a physician named Gary Brandwein.*

On June 27, 2007, Albany DA David Soares issued a statement confirming that Chris Benoit was a Signature customer:

> Obtaining illegal steroids has become effortless. What was once only available in gyms and through underground distribution channels is now available in the living rooms and bedrooms of anyone with access to the internet. All one must do is perform a quick search for their drug of choice and shop for the lowest cost distributor.
>
> Steroids are dangerous, can cause violent side effects and more needs to be done to ensure these drugs and other controlled substances are regulated, and do not end up in the hands of anyone, adults or children, without a valid prescription.
>
> After learning about the tragic deaths over the weekend, we were able to confirm that professional wrestler Christopher Benoit received packages from Signature Pharmacy and "wellness clinic" MedXlife.

---

* The indictment of Signature's owners was dismissed on technicalities in September 2008, but nine other defendants had already pleaded guilty.

Our thoughts are with the friends and loved ones of the Benoit family. . . .

The news of Benoit and Signature came at the same time WWE attorney McDevitt was insisting to the media, "There's no question [that] none of these drugs came from Internet pharmacies."

The Benoit-Signature connection also lessened the shock when, in August, names of other WWE stars surfaced on Albany DA lists of the pharmacy's customers. The most frequently cited list of WWE people was *Sports Illustrated*'s, which included Benoit; the others were Chavo Guerrero, John Hennigan ("Johnny Nitro"), Ken Anderson ("Mr. Kennedy"), Shoichi Funaki, Brian Adams (retired and soon dead), Charlie Haas, Eddie Fatu ("Umaga"), Adam Copeland ("Edge"), and Sylvain Grenier. Another list, in the *New York Daily News*, added six more: Randy Orton, Robert Huffman ("Booker T"), Shane Helms, Mike Bucci, Anthony Carelli ("Santino Marella"), and Darren Matthews ("William Regal"). (The Signature list also included, in much smaller numbers, baseball and football players, boxers, and entertainers.)

In an August 30 statement, WWE said that based on "independent information" from Albany investigators, "WWE has today, under the penalty provisions of its wellness policy, issued suspension notices to ten of its performers for violations. It has been WWE 's practice not to release the names of those who have been suspended, but notice has been sent to all WWE performers that names of anyone who is suspended under the wellness policy as of November 1 will be made public."

It was left to the obsessive students of TV story lines to match up the identities of the suspended wrestlers with those named in the press reports. The most curious case was Orton, a star of the very top tier who had a history of disciplinary issues and suspensions. His TV "push" continued unabated, so it was obvious he was not being suspended, and within weeks he headlined a pay-per-view show and recaptured a championship. If any of the earlier Orton suspensions had been for violations of the wellness policy, rather than general misbehavior, then the policy would have called for an escalating punishment for a second "strike" or termination for a third. Since WWE wasn't commenting on individual cases, the guess was that the company ruled that the publication of his name on the Signature lists was for an earlier violation for which he had already been punished. Another guess was just that WWE applied the wellness policy with blatant, self-serving inconsistency.

If Orton constituted a head-scratcher, the finger pointed at Mr. Kennedy — who *was* part of the August 30 group of suspensions — had to be marked hilarious. During the Benoit media frenzy, Kennedy/Anderson had been one of the most vociferous defenders of WWE on his blog and in televised interviews. In particular, he ridiculed the credentials of former WWF star Mero, saying Mero was unqualified to comment on conditions in wrestling in 2007. (Like Kennedy, Matthews/Regal and Guerrero also had lied during that period by maintaining they were clean, but neither was as obnoxious as Kennedy or as aggressive toward critics such as Mero.) Little more than a month later, Kennedy was shown to have been ordering anastrozole, among other drugs, through Signature. The certified use for anastrozole is for women fighting breast cancer. The "off-label" use for men is combating gynecomastia or enlarged mammaries — or, as they call it in the gyms, "bitch tits."*

***

On July 17, 2007, the Georgia Bureau of Investigation released the toxicology reports on the Benoit family. Before being killed, Daniel had been sedated with Xanax. Nancy's test showed Xanax, painkillers, and a high blood-alcohol level. And Chris had testosterone in his system — enough to give him a testosterone-to-epitestosterone ratio (T/E) of 59-to-1. Normal is 1-to-1. In Olympic drug testing, the cutoff was 4-to-1. In WWE drug testing, the cutoff was 10-to-1. According to Dave Meltzer, who also covered mixed martial arts, for which many state athletic commissions conduct drug tests, Benoit's T/E reading would have been the third-highest ever recorded in the California commission's thousands of tests of mixed martial artists and boxers.

But Dr. Kris Sperry, the state medical examiner, refused to go there. "We analyzed the urine of Chris Benoit for the presence of steroids, and the only steroid drug that we found was testosterone. This was measured at a level of 207 micrograms per liter," Sperry said blandly.

WWE lawyer McDevitt praised Sperry for conducting his press conference "very professionally and surgically." All the "speculation about the impact of steroids on this case was essentially removed by Dr. Sperry in about as clear a scientific language as one can articulate," McDevitt asserted. The key finding was that there were

---

* In 2009, WWE released Anderson/Kennedy, whose career was plagued by injuries.

"no illegal anabolic steroids" in Chris Benoit's body.

By the same logic, a heroin addict who obtained a hospital's supply of opium likewise would not manifest the presence of "illegal drugs." The Benoit and Toffoloni families hardly slept better knowing that what the toxicology tests most immediately identified as the cause of Chris's 59-to-1 T/E ratio was just testosterone, and not some common street drug.*

David Black, WWE's drug-testing administrator, said on CNN's *Nancy Grace* that if someone is on testosterone replacement therapy (and Black later confirmed that Benoit was), "the T/E ratio in the urine is no longer of interest. The interest and focus now shifts to the blood testing. And the T/E ratio, as someone takes testosterone replacement therapy, their body stops producing epitestosterone. . . . Testosterone's in the numerator. Epitestosterone's in the denominator. You can get a T/E ratio of infinity, and it does not mean anything."

In an interview for this book, Dr. Richard Auchus — an endocrinologist at the University of Texas Southwestern Medical Center in Dallas, who helped develop the therapeutic use exemption standards for the United States Anti-Doping Agency, the agency authorized by Congress to support the U.S. Olympic movement — disagreed.

"It is possible to be doping with a testosterone-to-epitestosterone ratio of 4-to-1," Auchus said. "It is impossible *not* to be doping with a T/E of 59-to-1."

---

* A facsimile of the Georgia Bureau of Investigation's news release on the toxicology report (undated but released on July 12, 2007) is included in the companion disk. See "Order the DVD" at the back of this book.

CHAPTER 13

Congress Cuts a Promo

ON JULY 6, 2007, REPRESENTATIVE Cliff Stearns, a Florida Republican, called for a Congressional investigation of "allegations of rampant steroid use in professional wrestling." Stearns said in a press release:

> Between 1985 and 2006, 89 wrestlers have died before the age of 50. Of course, not all of these deaths can be attributed to steroid use. However, this abnormally high number of deaths of young, fit athletes should raise congressional alarms. Millions of young wrestling fans, for better or for worse, look up to professional wrestlers as role models. The Anabolic Steroid Act of 1990 makes it a felony to use and distribute these drugs. Congress needs to investigate the recent events and find out how big of a problem steroid use is in professional wrestling. Steroid use is a major public health problem that deserves Congress' full attention.*

---

* FoxSports.com columnist Mark Kriegel noted at the time that Stearns' statistics were lifted from the appendix of my book *Wrestling Babylon*.

As chair of the Commerce, Trade and Consumer Protection Subcommittee of the House Committee on Energy and Commerce, Stearns in 2005 had conducted hearings for legislation he called the Drug Free Sports Act, which would have established a single testing standard for pro sports and set up a "three strikes" progression of punishments for violators, culminating in a lifetime ban. The bill stalled, and with the takeover by Democrats of majority control of the House of Representatives following the 2006 elections, the chairmanship of the subcommittee passed to Bobby Rush of Illinois.

Now the subcommittee's ranking minority member, Stearns joined the Benoit cable news yak-a-thon. The same month, former wrestler George Caiazzo ("John Kronus"), a star at Extreme Championship Wrestling in the 1990s, died at age thirty-eight in the usual sudden and mysterious way. Including Chris and Nancy Benoit, Caiazzo was the industry's seventh death in a thirty-day period.* Weeks later, Brian Adams, whose most prominent role had been as "Crush" in the old WWF tag team Demolition, died at forty-four of an overdose of painkillers and antidepressants. Adams also was a heavy steroid user; even in retirement, his name was found by prosecutors on the Signature Pharmacy customer list.

In August, Stearns visited the Funking Conservatory, a wrestling school in his Ocala, Florida, district, which was owned and operated by former pro wrestling star Dory Funk Jr. On the school's web TV show, the congressman was named a recipient of the Funking Conservatory

---

* Maybe the strangest was the self-hanging in Pittsburgh — an apparent copycat suicide — of independent wrestler James Fawcett ("Devil Bhukakan"), thirty-one, who idolized Benoit.

Fighting Heart Award and presented with a pair of wrestling boots signed by Funk. Perhaps that was what the congressman was after all along. With no leverage to force hearings, anyway, minus the active support of Chairman Rush, Stearns soon relinquished his ranking position on Commerce, Trade and Consumer Protection for the same spot on the Telecommunications and Internet Subcommittee.

Inevitably, Congressional investigations of wrestling would take a back seat to the public's superior fascination with steroid scandals in legitimate sports. The post-Benoit atmosphere on Capitol Hill reflected this push-pull dynamic. Important developments in the baseball steroid story — whether the November 2007 indictment of home-run king Barry Bonds for lying to a federal grand jury or the report to Major League Baseball the next month by former Senator George Mitchell — either could create a rising tide of attention for the wrestling sidebar, or bury it.

The campaign by the executive branch against steroid traffickers was already drawing the connections between real sports, "sports entertainment," and the unregulated marketing of "wellness" products to amateur jocks, youth chasers, and the otherwise vain and foolish. But the public education process was never about logic so much as it was about the ability of politicians to get a rub from proximity to celebrity hooks and themes. Thus, when baseball's Roger Clemens challenged the Mitchell Report finding that he had been injected with growth hormone by his personal trainer, Brian McNamee, and demanded a forum for clearing his name, Congressman Henry Waxman's House Committee on Oversight and Government Reform had the perfect vehicle. In February

2008 Clemens and McNamee testified before the Waxman committee, and a global Internet TV audience, with competing accounts of the former's familiarity with the needle and the damage done. Clemens wound up suing McNamee for defamation. The Justice Department wound up investigating Clemens for perjury.

Congressman Rush's subcommittee of Commerce and Energy, which felt the steroid issue was more appropriately under its direct legislative purview, fired back later in the month with an omnibus hearing on steroids and sports at which the heads of the major team sports and their players' unions said their pieces. Rush had wanted to include WWE, too. In November he emailed a *Baltimore Sun* reporter, "Given recent developments — the impending Mitchell report and reports of widespread abuse in professional wrestling — I believe it's time we get a formal update on what progress is being made to eradicate steroids from all sports and sports entertainment." Vince McMahon, however, declined the invitation to appear at the Rush subcommittee hearing on February 27, 2008. McMahon explained that his lawyer, Jerry McDevitt, was unavailable to accompany him that day.

"I am exceptionally and extremely disappointed," Rush said. Steroid abuse in pro wrestling "is probably worse than in any professional sport or amateur sport. . . . The number of deaths in the professional wrestling ranks is startling to say the least. The tragedy of Chris Benoit has been well documented. I want to assure Mr. McMahon that this committee fully intends to deal with the illegal steroid abuse in professional wrestling. And we hope he will be part of the solution and not part of the problem."

While Rush harrumphed, what the public didn't

know was that Congressional scrutiny of WWE had already played itself out behind the scenes. For all practical purposes, the game was over. In the last four months of 2007, McMahon and others from his organization were interviewed privately by counsel and investigators of the Waxman committee. That body would never issue a formal report. Instead, Waxman released his personal findings another full year later.

**

Despite being injected with exhibits totaling nearly a thousand pages, the Waxman report was not a report, but only a letter, dated January 2, 2009, to John Walters, director of the President's Office of National Drug Control Policy. The committee did not promulgate legislative recommendations or otherwise act on the basis of the chairman's letter. Given the constitutionally designed tension between the White House and the legislative branch under the principle of separation of powers, the Waxman letter was most deferential. Noting that he would soon be moving from Oversight and Government Reform to the chairmanship of another committee, Energy and Commerce, Waxman launched a booming punt to Walter: "I want to provide you with information from the Oversight Committee's investigation into the use of steroids in professional wrestling, which over three million children and teens watch regularly. I also request that your office examine the systematic deficiencies in the testing policies and practices of professional wrestling that the investigation has found."

The supplements consisted of transcripts of interviews by committee staff with WWE executives Vince and Linda McMahon and their daughter Stephanie McMahon Levesque, and with consultants contracted to support the WWE wellness program.* The committee also questioned Dixie Carter, owner of the much smaller Total Nonstop Action Wrestling, and published data on TNA's drug-testing.

The history of WWE testing fell into three periods. In 1987, two wrestlers, The Iron Sheik and Hacksaw Jim Duggan, were pulled over by New Jersey state troopers and arrested, the former for cocaine possession and the latter for marijuana. The incident, embarrassing on its face for WWF, was made worse by the status of the busted performers as, respectively, a heel and a babyface engaged in a story line feud and therefore, by the code of kayfabe, not supposed to be seen fraternizing. McMahon later explained the origin of company drug testing this way to the House committee staffers: "The first policy was generally put in place because it was perceived, and I believe accurately so, that we had a cocaine problem. And it was the '80s and a lot of people were engaged in that kind of party atmosphere. That is the reason why. I don't even know if we tested for steroids in that first policy or not." McMahon didn't add the joke among the talent of that period: "You're suspended if you test positive for cocaine or negative for steroids."

In 1991, following the prosecution of Dr. Zahorian's Pennsylvania steroid farm, WWF undertook the second

---

* In this book, the terms "wellness policy" and "wellness program" are used interchangeably. I intend "policy" in reference to the company's formulation and publication of a plan, and "program" in reference to how it operates, but the distinctions are trivial.

iteration of its drug-testing program, targeting banned anabolics. Zahorian's trial revealed the shipments of packages by Zahorian to many wrestlers who testified at the trial, as well as to McMahon and Hulk Hogan, who didn't. McMahon himself admitted to brief "experimentation" with the steroid Deca-Durabolin (nandrolone), after apparently having been turned on to it by Hogan during the filming of his flop *No Holds Barred*, wwf's first Hollywood feature.

For four years, wwe consulted on its new protocols with Dr. Mauro DiPasquale, a Canadian doctor who was such an authority on drug-testing technicalities that his 1987 book, *Drug Use & Detection in Amateur Sports*, was an underground classic used by steroid freaks to figure out ways to beat the system. David Black — a Ph.D. in pharmacological forensics who had spun off his lab on the Vanderbilt University campus into Aegis Analytical Laboratories, Inc., a for-profit contractor for sports leagues and law enforcement agencies — handled the specimen analysis.

A couple of top names from that period, The Ultimate Warrior and the British Bulldog (Davey Boy Smith), were terminated, though the lack of transparency in such cases always raised suspicion that running afoul of drug tests was the pretext rather than the reason for the dismissal.

But by 1996 the Zahorian-fueled scrutiny of wrestling had faded, and so had the wwf drug policy. McMahon was losing millions of dollars and his dominant pro wrestling market share in fierce competition with wcw. Top talent was jumping to wcw for both higher pay and the lure of a drug-testing apparatus even weaker than wwf's. So in an October 25, 1996, company memorandum, McMahon announced, "wwf, effective immediately, is suspending drug testing and collection on a group basis." He said the incidence of illegal and performance-enhancing drugs had become "so slight that group testing is no longer cost effective or necessary." The promotion reserved the right "to test any individual any time for the use of illegal substances"; such testing would proceed in a handful of cases, "for cause." In his interview with Congressional investigators, McMahon explained "cause" as "if someone were tardy consistently, if they missed dates, if they would fall asleep when they're not supposed to fall asleep. Any aberrant behavior, I think, would have been, in all likelihood, a reason, a probable reason to test."

The third and current version of the policy, the wellness program, was formulated after the November 2005 death of Eddie Guerrero. Linda McMahon conceded this obvious link; Vince maintained that he had begun developing the program "prior to Eddie's untimely demise." David Black's lab was brought back with an expanded role, though still only an administrative one, if not a clerical one — certainly one lacking the autonomous authority to interpret positive test results and impose penalties. This became evident when committee staff asked Black about wwe's failure to suspend Randy Orton after his name showed up in the summer of 2007 on the Signature Pharmacy list. Black said, "Oh, sure, I would agree that that's not good."

As the program evolved, Dr. Tracy Ray, a physician with the famous Birmingham, Alabama, sports medicine clinic of Dr. James Andrews, was engaged as the "medical review officer" to help make determinations on therapeutic use exemptions. Like Black's lab, though, Ray issued recommendations, not binding decisions. Still later, Dr. Frederick Feuerbach, a cardiologist, added heart tests. The Oversight Committee examined all these aspects of the WWE wellness program.

***

The *pièce de résistance* of the Waxman paper blizzard was the 122-page transcript of the committee staff's December 14, 2007, interview of Vince McMahon in the Rayburn House Office Building lounge. In that session, the WWE chairman was, by turns, bullying, self-pitying, creatively evasive, and utterly in character.

Earlier in the year, as WWE came under the microscope of the two Congressional committees, McMahon did a TV skit in which he compared these authorities to Barney Fife, the bumbling deputy sheriff portrayed by Don Knotts on the old Andy Griffith sitcom. Though dated, this was a favorite pop-culture image of McMahon's son-in-law, Triple H, whose wife, Stephanie, came in behind it in a backstage pep talk to the wrestlers. She bucked up the nervous talent by assuring them that Vince was not worried at all. In fact, Stephanie said, he planned to wear a clown wig at the eventual hearing.

McMahon's brazen December interview was not a formal hearing. His disdain for the investigators there fell just short of the mocking tactic Stephanie had promised, and the act would not have played as well live in public and on C-SPAN. But lawyer McDevitt and WWE lobbyists had worked to ensure favorable ground rules.

"Per our discussion with Jerry beforehand, we've not alerted the media," senior investigator Brian Cohen said near the beginning of the session. "Our intention was that you were able to come in here without having a media circus."

In lieu of a media circus, McMahon and McDevitt presented a two-person private circus. The latter objected on points large and small. The former was smug and smarmy.

When senior investigative counsel David Leviss recited routine language seeking confirmation that the interviewee was not using a recording device, McDevitt bristled: "Why would you even think we would do that? What good-faith basis would you even have to ask a question like that, whether we're recording this. We know it's against the rules. . . . I'm stunned by your question."

McMahon chimed in, "Are you guys recording any of this, other than the stenographer over here, in terms of television or radio." No. "Just thought I would ask."

The stage was set for the most aggressive wise guy act since Joe Pesci in *Goodfellas*.

"What is your current position with the company?" Leviss asked.

"Do we have to go through this rigmarole? Why don't you just get to the meat of it? You know who I am," McMahon replied.

A Republican campaign contributor, McMahon joked, "Why is it Republican [committee members' staffers] are smiling and the Democrats aren't?"

He said he didn't want to be penalized for WWE's problems: "We have problems sometimes because of the nature of our business, you know, that require things to be fixed. I had a double quad tear on both legs. You're sympathetic with that. Thank you. If only it were genuine."

He said he was looking forward to receiving "a gold star" from the committee for being so cooperative. On a follow-up question, he wanted to know if the investigators were "trying to slap my wrists." Committee counsel said they were just trying to understand a complex subject. "Great," McMahon said. "Thank you very much. I don't want you to spank me on the butt either."

He took umbrage at being asked his opinion of the possible long-term effects of steroids. "I'm not a doctor. I would suggest if I wanted to know long-term effects of any drug, I think the first place I would go is the FDA [Food and Drug Administration]. That would be the first place I would go. And, quite frankly, I don't think the FDA tells anyone about the long-term effects of steroid usage or abusage. And I would suggest to you that that might be someplace where your committee and Mr. Waxman, since you have oversight over these areas, might want to begin."

Had McMahon's company ever sought an expert medical opinion on this question? "No."

McMahon insisted that the chief target of the wellness policy was not steroids but the abuse of other prescription drugs. "There were a number of incidents in which, in the past, people have fallen asleep when they shouldn't, which would indicate that they were taking too many painkillers, things of that nature."

When McMahon was told that unnamed witnesses had expressed to the committee their view that WWE's business model relied on talent using "steroids or illegal drugs," McDevitt interjected: "Vince, don't even take these baits. You don't have to answer those kind of questions. We're not here to answer those. And if you think you can ever get a subpoena to ask questions like that, go ahead and try."

Why would accusers say such things? McMahon was asked. "Insanity," he said.

The committee staff tried to engage McMahon on two televised incidents in recent years in which wrestlers were taunted for looking smaller when they returned from drug suspensions. "As I recall," McMahon said dismissively, "there was one incident in which Triple H [made] an ad lib [to that effect]." There were actually two incidents. In one, Chris Masters was ridiculed by Triple H. In the other, Randy Orton was mocked by Vince McMahon.

Investigator Cohen noted that thirty WWE wrestlers tested positive for steroids or illegal drugs in 2006, and eleven in 2007. Between March 2006 and February 2007, fifteen were suspended, three received "TUE's," or therapeutic use exemptions, and twelve got "warnings." Cohen asked McMahon to "describe the circumstances under which those twelve wrestlers received warnings."

McDevitt: "You're basically asking him what he knows about the warning business? . . . Ask him about his conversation with Dr. Black, for Christ's sake. Come on, quit dancing."

McMahon added an oily, "I don't have anything to hide, guys. Just shoot me right between the eyes, okay?"

This led to a discussion of the initial concern of wrestlers over what would happen when they tested positive but had a doctor's prescription for steroids. McMahon said he eventually resolved the apparent confusion between Black and the wrestlers by hiring Dr. Ray, the medical review officer, to help determine the legitimacy of particular prescriptions and claims of TUE's.

"The nature of this policy is to do exactly what it was designed to do, the overall wellness of our talent," McMahon said. "Let's face it, as a good businessman, I don't want talent that isn't well. They can't perform. They can't perform at their highest level, and they won't be with us. So, obviously, I want talent to be healthy. Notwithstanding the fact that I am a human being and want other human beings to be healthy, aside from that, I'm a good businessman. I want my talent healthy, because if they're healthy, their clear longevity is much greater as intellectual property to the company. So, yeah, you know, I want this policy to be as good as it possibly can be."

McMahon disputed the idea that the wrestlers on the Signature Pharmacy list were caught by the Albany district attorney rather than by WWE. "My understanding, my recollection, okay, is of these eleven individuals identified by the Albany outfit . . . two of those had some sort of infraction with the testing with Dr. Black" — by which McMahon meant that they testified positive for something, whether or not it was the something they had illegally ordered from the Internet pharmacy.

McMahon said he took "great offense" to Waxman's statement at the time of the Signature revelations that the WWE policy deserved criticism because law enforcement, rather than the company, caught the miscreants. "It says to me, basically, that this is sort of a witch hunt kind of thing. You guys already have the answers before you even ask me the questions. . . . I think that is stupid, okay? That is out-and-out stupid. And I resent the fact that, you know, someone would fry us in the court of public opinion without having the knowledge you're now going to give [Waxman] based on my testimony. . . ."

On Chris Benoit specifically, McMahon revealed the misleading nature of company statements suggesting that Benoit's wellness program tests did not show steroid use. McMahon conceded that he didn't know when a test detected a banned substance, only when there was "a conclusion positive," which was the detection of a banned substance combined with Dr. Ray's conclusion that a TUE claim was invalid.

Some of the most convoluted dialogue involved an amendment to the WWE policy to cover wrestlers whose suspensions threatened to interrupt ongoing TV story lines. In August 2006, McMahon promulgated a policy change stating that the company "may, at its discretion, schedule the Talent to work selected televised events without pay and pay-per-views with pay during the 30 day suspension period." The theory was that sudden no-shows caused by last-minute suspensions penalized only the fans. By putting the offending wrestlers on TV for the purpose of resolving their story lines, WWE ensured that they were being punished, not rewarded; they were downgraded or forced to "do the honors" by losing out in their pending feuds.

How wrestlers got paid, in this or any circumstance, was almost impossible for an outsider to calculate. WWE pegged compensation to its own accountings of ticket sales and other revenue streams; the only stipulated payment by contract was $200 per television shoot. (The talent above the "jobber" or "enhancement" level had written into their contracts what were known as "downside guarantees" of annual income from these accountings.)

McMahon had this to say about why and how such suspensions were held in abeyance: "I'm resolving an issue on television, and I'm doing it very quickly. I'm doing it as quickly as we possibly can. . . . And, again, we're different than anybody else. We're not a sport, emphasize, okay. It's not like baseball or whatever else it may be and you're not playing, you're out for fourteen games or whatever it might be. This is entertainment. We are so different than sport. We are entertainment."*

McMahon was contemptuous of the idea that WWE bore any responsibility for the astounding early mortality rate of wrestlers. Asked about the Meltzer study showing the deaths of sixty-two performers under the age of fifty in WWE and other "major league" organizations (including WCW and the original ECW), McMahon said, "I'm not familiar with anything Dave Meltzer writes. He's a gossip columnist. I don't read what he has to write. Like I say, he's a dirt monger. There are a number of those. We call them dirt sheets and they have very little credibility."

In August 2007, Frank Deford, the author and *Sports Illustrated* writer, touted Meltzer's study in a National Public Radio commentary. Deford (who employed Meltzer as a wrestling columnist at the *National* in 1990–91 and on at least one occasion fended off pressure from McMahon to fire him) called Meltzer "the most accomplished reporter in sports journalism." McMahon was unimpressed. He said Deford carried a grudge against him over an incident in which the promoter made off with one of the writer's shoes after they went bowling at a country club.**

In the summer of 2007, WWE sent a letter to about 500 former wrestlers offering to underwrite the full costs of substance-abuse treatment because, as the letter put it,

---

* *Wrestling Observer*'s Meltzer pointed out the hypocrisy of WWE's professed concern for customers when the company adjusts wrestlers' suspensions in order to preserve story lines. The company often pulled star wrestlers from events in order to support story line injuries that didn't really happen — but not until fans had already purchased tickets thinking those wrestlers would be there.

** Deford confirmed this bizarre story, which took place at a birthday party

"Over the last ten years, an inordinate number of wrestlers have passed away. Some of those deaths may in part have been caused by drugs or alcohol." McMahon told the Congressional investigators that this was "unfortunately about the only thing that we can do. I don't like to read about these deaths at all. And some of these people who have overdosed and things of that nature have been friends of mine. It's upsetting on every conceivable front. So as a not necessarily a responsible, but I think I would like to throw in responsible as well, corporate member of society, notwithstanding again the fact I'm a human being, I don't know anything else we can do other than to extend that service or whatever to someone who may have a problem."

McMahon summarized his motivation for the letter to former talent by saying this: "Two words: public relations. That's it. I do not feel any sense of responsibility for anyone of whatever their age is who has passed along and has bad habits and overdoses for drugs. Sorry, I don't feel any responsibility for that. Nonetheless, that's why we're [reaching out with the letter]. It is a magnanimous gesture."

The committee staff asked whether McMahon himself, who had a talent contract and still stepped into the ring a couple of times a year, was subject to the wellness policy. The answer was no. "I'm not a regularly scheduled performer. In addition to that I'm sixty-two years old, not twenty-six. And the wellness policy is designed

---

for John Filippelli, a TV sports producer who at the time was coordinating TV operations for WWE. Pat Patterson, a retired wrestler who was then McMahon's right-hand man, stole one of Deford's shoes and one of his wife's. Patterson and McMahon found this hilarious. "I'm rather amazed McMahon brought this up, but it's a pretty accurate account of him acting like a horse's ass," Deford said in an email to me.

for those young competitors who compete on a regular basis."

Had McMahon used steroids since his admitted use in the '90s?

"I'm not going to allow you to harass this man," McDevitt exploded. "How is that pertinent to anything about whether this wellness program works? And you came in here today professing you have an open mind and you're telling me that you didn't have this in mind when you [earlier shared a list of anticipated questions]? Bullshit."

"I'm refusing to answer the question," McMahon confirmed.

***

Congressman Waxman summarized his views in the letter to John Walters, the White House drug policy director. Waxman reported that "baseline testing," at the beginning of the program in March 2006, found forty percent of WWE's 186 wrestlers testing positive despite advance warning.

Then there were the TV and pay-per-view non-suspension suspensions.

There was the evidence that WWE, in 2007–08, went on to hire four out of the five wrestlers who tested positive for steroids in pre-contract testing. The only one not hired was the one who tested positive for both steroids *and* cocaine.

There were the TUE's, tied to a circular "testosterone replacement acceptance program" for wrestlers who had damaged their endocrinological systems with past steroid abuse. Dr. Ray, who had made the recommendations affirming seven TUE's, conceded in his interview that "there was shadiness in almost every case that I've reviewed."

In the summer of 2007, WWE had contacted Dr. Richard Auchus, the Southwestern Medical Center and anti-doping agency endocrinologist (who is quoted at the end of the preceding chapter), about working with WWE on TUE standards. In the December interview on Capitol Hill, McMahon said he was "considering" and "contemplating" such a move. Ultimately, Auchus's two-page proposal for getting past steroid abusers off androgens — a plan he compared to using methadone to wean heroin addicts — was dropped. (In October 2008 WWE would hire a different endocrinologist, Dr. Vijay Bahl of the University of Pittsburgh Medical Center, but the announcement said nothing specific about TUE's.)

Finally, Chris Benoit. "According to WWE officials, Mr. Benoit was tested four times for steroids prior to his death. He tested positive three times, but each time he received only a warning or no penalty at all. The Committee obtained no evidence that efforts were made to discourage his steroid abuse," the Waxman letter noted.

Waxman's documentation seemed to be an attempt, in the absence of public hearings, to close the loop on an unresolved topic. The chance that anything substantive would come out of it, in terms of regulation or serious pressure on WWE to make its drug-testing apparatus truly independent, was low. Eighteen months after the Benoit murders, Congress had made a little bit of noise about the problem but left almost no imprint on a possible solution.

***

On Election Eve, November 3, 2008, the two major pres-
idential candidates, Barack Obama and John McCain,
were interviewed at halftime of ESPN's *Monday Night
Football*. Each was asked to name the reform in sports
that would be his priority if the voters chose him the
next day.

Living up to his image as an old-fashioned moralist,
McCain said he would work to eliminate steroids in
sports.

Obama vowed to advocate to replace the current
Bowl Championship Series with a credible playoff system, which every year would guarantee the nation an
undisputed national college football champion.

CHAPTER 14

All the World's a Stooge

CERTAIN DROLL APHORISMS about pro wrestling, if delivered by men in tweed rather than spandex, would be recognized staples of academic deconstruction theory. For example, the wrestler-promoter Cowboy Bill Watts once confronted the topic of the sport's fake nature with this puzzler: "Work or shoot — either way, it's still a competition." Watts meant that just because "sports entertainment" is physical theater rather than a legitimate contest doesn't change the fact that one participant is trying to get the upper hand over the other under some admittedly elusive standard. Or anyway, that's *probably* what Watts meant. Michel Foucault took the final three-count in 1984. The absence of a pulse got Roland Barthes disqualified from life in 1980. Neither could be consulted.

You can't talk to a man with a shotgun in his hand. Nor can you argue with anyone who thinks a cluster of avoidable deaths, in a show business in a non-war zone, can be rationalized. Vince McMahon knows this; the rest of us only suspect it. Chris Benoit might have snapped — but the ring ropes guarding his way of life from reality did not.

233

They just got a little more frayed. They will snap next time, or the time after that. Or they won't. In the Western Canada and American South of Benoit, in the New Jersey of Mickey Rourke's Randy "The Ram" Robinson in *The Wrestler*, and at all points in between, young men (and women) are still taking, and will always take, to extremes their ambition to bask in the roar of the crowd. As a society, we have decided that the collective price they pay is OK. Similarly, we have decided not to make that big a deal of the inevitability of a "student-athlete" croaking every now and then at a "voluntary" off-season college football practice.

***

Chris killed Nancy on Friday night, Daniel either very late Friday or some time Saturday, and himself on Sunday morning. What happened?

Most likely, Chris and Nancy had their final fight, spontaneously, and it got out of hand. A false dichotomy of the subsequent debate over steroids was that acts of deliberation across a several-day period could not have been the result of "roid rage." Such a framing of the events misses two things. One is that the first murder, Nancy's, could very well have been produced by a quick burst of rage, with the other acts being ones of greater calculation — more like desperation — once Chris realized what he had done.

The other thing missed by harping on the 'roid rage straw man is more fundamental: steroids also can cause depression. Whether or not they were the main cause of the crime, steroids and the steroid culture were an important factor.

WWE counted on the enormous capacity of its fans to deny and the enormous capacity of everyone else to shrug. At strategic points, it rolled out the sound bites it needed, such as when beloved TV announcer and former company executive Jim Ross attended the funeral of Nancy and Daniel at Our Lady of Lourdes Catholic Church in Daytona Beach, Florida, on July 14, 2007. "This is not a steroid issue," Ross told the media. "That horse has got to be put in the barn and unsaddled."

Those who read the Georgia medical examiner's toxicology report, which was released three days later, might have been tempted to get back in the saddle. But not good old "JR."

***

The presence of a small amount of Nancy's blood indicated that Chris banged her head on the floor in the course of a struggle, which, if he were serious, could not have lasted long. "Some type of violence" was evident, the sheriff's report said, including "several impact injuries to her head, and possibly to her body, but it is unclear what type of instrument or object caused the injuries." Why Chris then felt the need to tie up Nancy, either before or after killing her, takes us to the outer reaches of speculation. One theory is that he considered the possibility of fleeing with Daniel, or in any case somehow making the scene look like a third-party home-invasion crime.

During the dispute between the Benoit and Toffoloni families over the disposition of the estate, a question arose about the order of the deaths. Neither Chris nor Nancy left a will, and the answer had implications under a Georgia slayer statute, whereby the estate claims of a murderer are forfeited. The law would have kicked in if the Toffolonis could establish, as they suggested they would, that Chris killed Daniel first, and Nancy's side could argue for a larger share of the assets.

A handwritten document in the files of the Toffolonis' lawyer, Richard Decker, headed "Leigh's theory," outlined one possible scenario. (I asked Decker who Leigh was. "Don't know for sure, probably one of our paralegals," Decker emailed back.) Leigh's notes:

Friday night — all 3 seen at pool

Nobody seen Saturday

Later Fri. maybe Saturday morning Nancy and Chris fight over drugs or some other issue and Chris, all jacked up on his stuff from Astin, hits Nancy on the head and knocks her out, maybe an accident. She had many central nervous system depressants in her system to enforce the unconsciousness. This would explain why Chris tied her up, to keep her contained while he figures out what to do. Daniel finds out what happens and freaks out. Chris sedates Daniel to calm him down but accidentally gives him too much and he dies.

Xanax peak plasma concentration about 1 hr after administration. At this point he loses his mind completely and goes to the office and kills Nancy.

Doesn't make any sense that he would kill Daniel first, chances are he killed Daniel accidentally, to sedate him, gave him too much and died so at that point he knew he was in too deep. While in contact with WWE they may have still been alive, after they told him not to show up Sat he got scared his career over and decided to end it hence leaving the drugs out to be found

Nancy still had alcohol in her blood, why did no other bodies produce alcohol during decomposition

It must be reemphasized that this theory appears to have been drawn up to advance a particular monetary interest. (The theory became moot when the Benoits and the Toffolonis settled the estate dispute by splitting the assets right down the middle, abandoning any claim the latter might have been contemplating of their entitlement to a larger share.) The theory means little more than that. The narrative of any crime, especially one with no surviving witnesses, has open-ended elements. Here the open-endedness was worsened by the poor record created by the authorities.

***

Since the summer of 2007, Atlanta's dubious distinction as a capital of wrestling's drug culture hasn't missed a beat. On March 23, 2008, thirty-four-year-old ex-wrestler Chase Tatum was found dead in his Atlanta home from an overdose of painkillers. Two weeks earlier, Tatum had been recovering from surgery for a degenerative spinal disc. He was a heavy-duty steroid guy at wcw in the '90s.

The next month the daughter of a preacher in another Atlanta suburb, Locust Grove, came across a stash of at least eight vials of steroids, testosterone, and growth hormone, and more than twenty syringes, in their house attic. The drugs were left by former residents of the house, who included WWE wrestler Michael Hettinga ("Mike Knox"). Hettinga's WWE contract and a company memorandum about its dress code were also found.

***

In 2008 director Christopher Bell released the critically acclaimed documentary *Bigger Faster Stronger*, which glorified his own steroid use and that of his brothers Mark and Mike.

On December 14, 2008, "Mad Dog" Mike Bell, who wrestled for both WWE and the original ECW, was found dead at Ramona House, a substance abuse rehabilitation facility in Costa Mesa, California. He was thirty-seven.

***

On January 16, 2009, independent wrestler Paul Fuchs ("Paul E. Normus"), who had a cameo role in the even more critically acclaimed dramatic film *The Wrestler*, was found dead at his parents' home in Sloatsburg, New York. Fuchs was thirty-three.

***

Another character in *The Wrestler* was a drug dealer, portrayed by Scott Siegel. It was method acting at its finest, for Siegel was a real-life drug dealer. So exposing himself on the big screen could not have helped him elude the DEA agents who were closing in on him.

As the website TMZ.com reported on February 19, 2009:

> Scott Siegel was already under DEA surveillance in Westchester County, NY last night when officers spotted him picking up a package. Feds in four cars moved in, and the raging beefcake allegedly rammed three of their cars — then took off on foot.
>
> Officers caught up with Scott and arrested him for steroid distribution and assaulting a federal officer.
>
> UPDATE: Siegel's bail has just been denied — due to strong evidence against him, along with his 1999 conviction for selling steroids.

* * *

A handful of ex-WWE wrestlers took up Vince McMahon's offer to underwrite alcohol and substance rehab. One of them, Jake "The Snake" Roberts, expressed his undying gratitude before he and his prop, a live cobra, headed back out to independent bookings.

Another old druggie, Lanny Kean, "Cousin Junior" in the '80s, checked out early, from his rehab clinic and then from life. On January 12, 2009, Kean suffered a fatal heart attack in Jamestown, Kentucky. He was forty-eight.

* * *

Early in 2007, months before the Benoit rampage, WWE star Andrew Martin failed a wellness program test and was suspended. He was released soon thereafter. Martin was known as "Test." The handle was an inside joke about drug-testing.

Martin — also at one time the boyfriend of WWE diva Barbara Blank ("Kelly Kelly") — became a part-time independent wrestler. In April 2007 the Maryland athletic commission refused to let Martin work his spot in a show because he was under the influence. He also missed numerous other bookings. After his April 2008 arrest for driving drunk and with a suspended license, he accepted WWE's offer to underwrite rehab. In August he checked himself into the Hanley Rehabilitation Center in West Palm Beach, Florida, for treatment of a painkiller addiction.

On March 13, 2009, a neighbor of Martin's at a water-front condo complex in Tampa saw through the balcony window that he had appeared to have been sitting in the same awkward position for more than twenty-four hours. The neighbor called police, who climbed a ladder to the balcony and entered the apartment through an open window. Martin was dead. Steroids and painkillers were found on the property. He was thirty-three.

∗∗∗

World Wrestling Entertainment put a lot of hours into the obliteration of all references to Chris Benoit in its DVDs. A few leaks remained, mostly in side references by announcers in non-Benoit matches.

On the June 28, 2007, *Today* show on NBC, Vince McMahon told Meredith Viera, "There was no way of telling this man was a monster."

Yet according to company sources, WWE privately held out hope that, over time, the "monster" of the tale would prove to be Nancy, Chris's image could be rehabilitated, and the marketing of his branded merchandise could resume. Some office flunkies were tasked with helping to bring about this happy day.

In the secondary market on eBay, all things Benoit moved briskly. Out of every three fans, one was creeped out by this, one wallowed in it, and a third experienced the latter while pretending to experience the former.

Shortly before his death, Chris Benoit gave Ray Rawls, the small-time wrestler who made his ring wear, a special token of their friendship: the dark tights with blue piping and design that Benoit wore when he won the championship at *WrestleMania* 2004. It was something he wanted to do for Rawls, Chris said. He added, "It's for your use in the future." Following the murder-suicide, and because of the loss of his star customer and other factors, Rawls was broke. Though he felt guilty doing so, Rawls decided that Chris had been giving him permission to auction the tights on eBay to keep the wolf from the door.

The tights fetched $3,000.

***

On May 12, 2009, Astin was sentenced to ten years in federal prison. The harsh sentence was dictated by information from the prosecutors that his promiscuous prescription practices had resulted in the deaths of at least two patients — two, that is, other than Chris and Nancy Benoit. (Though not named, both were believed to be ex-wrestlers: Johnny Grunge and "Sensational Sherri" Martel.)

On June 10, 2009, just before the statutory deadline for a civil wrongful-death lawsuit, Maureen and Paul Toffoloni

— the parents of Nancy Benoit and grandparents of Daniel — sued Astin, who was already headed to prison, along with unknown "Distributors X, Y, and Z." The Toffolonis sought damages stemming from Astin's actions as Chris's physician for seven years, The complaint charged that the doctor's misconduct put his patient "under the influence of CNS [central nervous system] depressants, opioids and anabolic and androgenic steroids," in turn impairing him mentally and triggering his homicidal-suicidal rampage. The family apparently was depending on subsequent revelations, during discovery and trial, to establish the identities of the co-defendants — "manufac-turers, distributors, wholesalers and/or retail sellers of certain anabolic and androgenic steroids, narcotic drugs and/or controlled substances."

WWE was not named.

***

Securities and Exchange Commission filings by World Wrestling Entertainment, Inc., disclosed $526.5 million in net revenues in 2008, broken down as follows:

Live and Televised Entertainment	$331.5 million
Consumer Products	$135.7 million
Digital Media	$34.8 million
WWE Studios	$24.5 million

About three-quarters of the revenues came from North America operations. Other portions were generat-ed in EMEA (Europe, Middle East, and Africa), 18%; APAC (Asia Pacific), 7%; and Emerging Markets (Latin America, China), 1%.

***

On January 12, 2009, Connecticut Governor M. Jodi Rell nominated Linda McMahon for a position on the state Board of Education.

Rell said, "Linda clearly understands the skills and education needed to succeed in business and the type of highly educated and skilled workforce that must be available to ensure that success. I am confident that her leadership abilities, input and advocacy as a mother and grandmother will be key assets to the Board and its mission of ensuring quality education for all Connecticut children."

During the confirmation process, McMahon acknowledged that her claim that she had a degree in education was false. She said the error on her resume was caused by honest confusion.

Linda McMahon was confirmed by the State Senate, 34–1, and by the House of Representatives, 96–45.

Notes on Sources

At the back of this book is information on how to order on disk some of the background records I used. The goal here was for as much transparency as possible. From the get-go, I had faith that, even if the Benoit crime itself flashed no conspiratorial smoking gun, a close reading of the public record would reveal more than we might think.

Below are the stories behind the stories of a few important aspects of my reporting.

FAYETTE COUNTY AUTHORITIES

On February 12, 2008, the Fayette County Sheriff's Office released a report closing the Benoit investigation. The materials consisted of a fifty-two-page case summary by Detective Ethon Harper, the lead investigator, along with more than 300 pages of supplemental reports and records.

Through the public information officer, Lieutenant Belinda McCastle, then-Sheriff Randall Johnson said that only Harper was authorized to talk to me; everyone else in the department was instructed to grant no interviews. I reached out to others as needed, but it was clear that the sheriff's employees took his directive seriously.

My dialogue with Harper started off amiably before quickly dribbling into nothingness. As the questions got sharper, Harper did not want to interpret the gaps in his report, which I was showing were not just discretionary, but passive to the point of negligence. Missing text messages, arbitrarily truncated phone call logs, absence of voicemail evidence, references to documents and records that were not released and then, in defense, were explained as never having existed at all — all these detours from openness and common sense speak for themselves.

"I hope you are keeping in mind that I am not a professional writer," Harper said at one point. Ultimately, his lack of felicity with the written word was presumed to excuse that where he represented that Scott Armstrong had said something "in a statement," the detective merely meant to refer to something he claimed to remember Armstrong stating. There was no backup document, after all; the plain language suggesting otherwise was a swerve.

In an April 8, 2008, email, Harper accused me of not publishing on my blog his explanation of a text message Armstrong sent to Chris Benoit on June 24, 2007. "I thought you said you did not want to 'hype,'" Harper wrote. When I replied that I had received no such explanation and asked him to show me the original message, he wrote back, "I clear out my sent box pretty frequently to keep from getting the 'over size limits' message from our server. I don't have any messages past a week ago." Unfortunately for his logic, such a message would have been less than a week earlier. Anyway, Harper wrote, "I was really just poking a little bit of fun at you. No reason to point out a misunderstanding and make it a bigger issue than it is."

If this was a joke, I wasn't laughing. Thereafter, Harper stopped returning phone calls, emails, and faxes.

Three months later came the search for the Stamford police interview of the Wikipedia hacker, which the Fayette County sheriff's report said was "included in the case file." After several rounds of dodgeball, Harper said, through sheriff's attorney Richard Lindsey, "We have had and still do have the video they sent us. The video cuts out after just a couple of minutes, so there is no recorded interview."* I demanded and received what was, in fact, a partial recorded interview. I asked Lindsey why the sheriff's office issued a report on this aspect of its investigation on such a basis. Lindsey wrote back, "I have no idea."

After a time-consuming fight that led all the way to the docket of the Connecticut Freedom of Information Commission, I got the full video from Stamford, and it reinforced the apparent determination of authorities in two states not to breathe a word of whatever was known about why the body of a famous wrestler — who was uncharacteristically missing appearances — and the bodies of his wife and their son could lie around decomposing for days.

Then there were the grudging and piecemeal releases of copies of WWE's calls to 911. All records "of the initial call to 911 for a welfare check may be obtained from the Fayette County 911 Communications Center," noted the summary of the open records. By omission, this at least implied the existence of only one 911 call. After I applied

---

* My email exchanges with Harper are included in the companion disk. See "Order the DVD" at the back of this book.

to the 911 center for "the" call and listened to it, it was evident that there were others; in fact, three iterations of requests to the center were required before the complete collection of *eight* audio records got pinned down.

At the beginning of the process, Lindsey had written to me, "I suggest that you read the investigator's summary first (which I am sending to you) to determine if you really need the 911 documents. The summary is very good."

Later Lindsey was angered by my persistent questions about the mysterious Scott Armstrong "statement." Unable to understand why Harper wouldn't produce what nine out of ten drunks in a bar could identify in that context as a dedicated document, I assured Lindsey that I would not make a fuss if such a document surfaced and turned out not to have been disclosed previously due to an honest mistake. Lindsey then threatened in an email, "If you ever imply that I withheld anything, all communication will cease immediately." He complained that he was "at the mercy" of his client in such a situation. "I do not withhold documents — I never have and never will. If I read that again (as a threat, comment or thought), you'll have to get a court order before I will ever communicate further with you." After I replied that I'd proferred no such threat, comment, or thought, Lindsey apologized.

MICHAEL BENOIT

Michael Benoit, Chris's father, contacted me early in 2008, after we were separately interviewed for a documentary on the Canadian Broadcasting Corporation program *the fifth estate*. Mike was most interested in promoting research suggesting that Chronic Traumatic

Encephalopathy — a doctor's neologism for the brain damage he had found caused by Chris's serial concussions in the ring — had been the central cause of his rampage. I promised Mike that I would cover and address this research respectfully, whereupon he wrote me, "I will help you with any details you require for your book. I will not ask that you write in a manner that is pro Chris Benoit."

For several months Mike and I conversed extensively, though at arm's length, in dozens of emails and several long phone conversations, about aspects of my reporting on the timeline in particular, and we contemplated meeting face to face for further conversations on a range of topics. Mike was eager to introduce me to one of the CTE research pioneers, Dr. Bennet Omalu, a professor at the University of California-Davis Medical School, the coroner of San Joaquin County, California, and the author of *Play Hard, Die Young: Football, Dementia, Depression and Death*. A meeting among the three of us almost happened in May 2008, when the producers of NBC's *Dateline* planned to fly Mike to San Jose to participate in interviews for an investigative piece. But Mike's flight was canceled at the last minute as NBC abruptly scrapped the Benoit story.

A month earlier Mike had been a key confirming source as I nailed down the story of WWE's phony *Raw* tribute show, hours after company executives knew full well that they were spinning a murder-suicide. After the publication of that report on my blog, Wrestling Babylon News (http://muchnick.net/babylon), he alerted me to a clumsy attempt to discredit me by Scott Zerr, an Edmonton journalist who had hoped to work with Chris on his autobiography. (Zerr might have been smearing me in concert with Carl DeMarco, the head of WWE's Canadian operations, who likely had been embarrassed by my revelation that the leak of the company's early knowledge that Chris was the killer came from DeMarco.) For details, see the April 6, 2008, posts on Wrestling Babylon News.

Mike and I never met in person, and he eventually cut off contact altogether. Though I found his information on Chris's brain trauma useful, I intuited a difference — one that I think Mike, grasping at straws to explain the criminal acts of his beloved son, couldn't accept — between it being a contributing factor and the single, comprehensive explanation for this tragedy. I later independently spoke to Dr. Omalu; and while I agreed that the concussion research was an important emerging field, certain to save the lives of future athletes, and that this deserved to be noted as part of Chris's legacy, I also felt that it was exaggerated by Dr. Omalu as well as by Mike. As a father, I empathized with Mike. But as a journalist, I had a job to do.

Along the way, before I got on his bad side, Mike put me in touch with the office of his lawyer, Cary Ichter. My reporting on gaps in the sheriff's account of the telephone records had spurred Mike to direct Ichter to hire technicians who combed Chris and Nancy's cell phones and computer for further insights into the weekend timeline and other issues. (I well understood that as we compared notes, Patricia Roy, one of Ichter's assistants, would get far more information from me than I from her; the statutory deadline for filing a civil lawsuit against WWE was several months after the completion of this book.)

As a member of the Georgia Athletic Commission, Ichter also was pushing for new legislation to regulate the pro wrestling industry there. I, too, strongly advocate regulation. Still, in this particular scenario I found myself thinking WWE officials had a point when they complained that a commission member who was also a lawyer contemplating a major lawsuit against the company in private practice had a blatant conflict of interest. The merits of Ichter's proposals, as opposed to their process, make for a more complex discussion; but in any case, they quickly foundered when WWE threatened to pull out of Georgia if toothful regulations were enacted.

In our few conversations, Ichter expressed interest in using my book to help promote a lawsuit by his client Carlos Ashenoff ("Konnan") against Total Non-Stop Action Wrestling. The suit alleged that the promotion negligently endangered Ashenoff by forcing him to work through debilitating injuries, which led to life-threatening transplant surgery after the wrestler's kidneys stopped functioning, most likely a consequence of toxic doses of painkillers. The case also included claims of racial discrimination, based on the stereotype Latino character that Ashenoff, a native Cuban, said he was forced to portray in order to maintain TNA employment. That count echoed a discrimination suit Ichter had filed years earlier against World Championship Wrestling on behalf of a group of African-American wrestlers, who won a substantial settlement. (In a well-known piece of wrestling lore, that settlement was driven by an extraneous factor: a report of racist comments by Bill Watts, who at the time was running WCW, reached baseball legend Hank Aaron, an executive with WCW's parent Turner Broadcasting System, and higher-ups quickly passed down orders to resolve quickly any disputes adversely impacting the company's image in race relations.)

I must say that, on intellectual principle, I am unimpressed by this type of racial-discrimination litigation in wrestling — which, after all, is a lowbrow entertainment form, by definition exploiting lowest-common-denominator gimmicks. I do not find risible the proposition that the legal system should set right the reality that racism (or homophobia or sexism or xenophobia) will always be a default ingredient of the recipe of fictional story lines. If Turner Broadcasting didn't want to be part of such a business, it could get out — and eventually it did.

In our conversations, Mike Benoit was the first to raise the point that his lawyer sometimes behaved "unprofessionally," as Mike put it. In one set of meetings Ichter "kept calling this person an 'asshole' and that person an 'asshole.' In my experience, when you're calling everyone else an asshole, maybe the first thing you should be doing is looking in the mirror," Mike said.

Late in 2007, Ichter leaked the story that the Benoits had offered to settle with WWE for $2 million. WWE rejected the offer and Mike Benoit denied ever having authorized it. Thereafter, he told me, he instructed Ichter to focus on estate matters only.

All of which is to emphasize that the thrust of this book is not willy-nilly wrestling-bashing. The real take-out here is the outrageously out-of-bounds health and safety risks in this industry, which — in the absence of a sensible regulatory regime — the talent must bear all by themselves.

HOLLY SCHREPFER

Naturally, I sought the cooperation of Holly Schrepfer. In March 2008 Mike Benoit told me that he had arranged for Schrepfer (often referred to in media reports as Holly McFague) to talk to me about the timeline of events following her discovery of the bodies. When I called her, though, I found that either Mike had misunderstood or she had developed second thoughts.

Specifically, Holly said she had addressed all of my questions about the subject in her official statement to the sheriff. Taken aback, I said I would thoroughly review her statement, which I'd already read, and call her back only if I still thought we had things to talk about.

When I did call back, Holly responded that from what I was telling her, the sheriff's release of records must have included only one of the four or five separate statements she said she'd given investigators. At that point I went back to Detective Harper, who flatly denied that there were additional, undisclosed Schrepfer statements. "You have what I have," Harper said.

Holly then conceded that, in the trauma of her involvement in these horrible events, she might have been confused about whether there were additional formal statements. But in any case she did not want to rehash things with me.

(In light of the detective's several subsequent false and misleading statements to me on other subjects — see above — I now suspect that there were, in fact, multiple undisclosed statements by Holly. These and other buried materials may surface in the Toffoloni's civil suit against Dr. Astin and "Distributors X, Y, and Z.")

Four months later, before traveling to Georgia for additional reporting, I checked in again with Holly. We had a pleasant chat, but she reiterated that I wouldn't get additional input from her. She felt that she had already said everything that needed to be said, to the authorities and to the families and their lawyers. The only thing that might motivate her to weigh in further publicly on timeline discrepancies, she said, would be evidence that if someone had taken more proactive steps with the very earliest and sketchiest information, Daniel Benoit's life might have been saved. I consider the timeline material in this book important for its own reasons, but I also think Holly is likely correct in her position that no evidence exists that anyone was in an effective position to intervene after Nancy's murder but before Daniel's.

SANDRA TOFFOLONI

Through intermediaries, I learned that Sandra Toffoloni, Nancy Benoit's sister, followed my blog and approved of my search for deeper levels of the truth. There was, however, one exception: she didn't like my refusal to bury the early reports that Daniel Benoit had Fragile X syndrome. For Sandra, this may have been a version of Mike Benoit's dissatisfaction with my lack of emphasis on Chris's mental impairment from concussions. I was, and remain, respectful of what both families have gone through, and of their interests in preserving positive memories of their loved ones. But, for me, telling the complete story involved resolving all angles, including Daniel's, in an accurate fashion.

In the spring and summer of 2008, I exchanged a few friendly emails with Sandra as she organized the launch of the Nancy and Daniel Benoit Foundation, "dedicated to preventing steroid abuse through education and raising awareness about the unfortunate effects steroids can have on users and those close to them." In vague terms, we talked about chatting on the phone in greater depth.

On July 5, 2008, my wife answered a phone call from Sandra at 1 a.m. in California — which was 4 a.m. at her home in North Carolina. My wife chose to take a message rather than wake me. In an email the next day, Sandra explained that as a professional event planner she had a tendency to keep odd hours and lose track of the best time to call people. Sandra again said she would talk with me at the appropriate time. "I firmly believe there is responsibility to be taken, not just by Christopher," Sandra wrote.

I followed up with more overtures to schedule a phone discussion, but Sandra did not respond.

On January 23, 2009, Nancy Benoit's friend Pam Hildebrand Clark told me that Sandra Toffoloni had authorized her to give me her cell phone number. I left a message for Sandra at that number, and she called me back and we talked about a few points in the book. We made an appointment for a second and longer conversation, but she did not keep it.

JERRY McDEVITT AND THE BLOG RETRACTION

In the spring of 2008 I corresponded with Gary Davis, World Wrestling Entertainment's vice president of corporate communications, with questions about timeline discrepancies. In his second and last email to me, on April 1, Davis said, "I recognize you have an interest in this subject, but why are you asking for this information, how do you intend to use this information if it is provided, and what is it that you think this information, if provided, is going to prove?"

From June 16 through June 18, 2008, WWE's chief outside counsel, Jerry S. McDevitt, emailed me a series of legal threats; those messages and my responses to them were published on my blog.

One of my blog posts erroneously suggested that McDevitt had misled the public by insisting that WWE acted within days in the summer of 2007 to suspend company performers who were revealed to be on the customer list of an Internet steroid connection, Signature Pharmacy, under investigation by the district attorney of Albany, New York. My assertion that WWE had waited more than two weeks before suspending the talent who had violated the company's wellness policy relied on a report by Dave Meltzer's *Wrestling Observer*. Investigating McDevitt's complaint, I concluded that Meltzer was wrong in that detail, and I ran a retraction on my blog. Later conversations with Christopher Baynes of the Albany DA's office and Mark Haskins of the New York State Narcotic Enforcement Agency confirmed McDevitt's chronology of the WWE suspensions.*

For Meltzer's part, I believe he exercised poor journalistic judgment by neither correcting the item himself nor informing his readers of my dispute with McDevitt — which, after all, had arisen out of my straightforward citation of a prominent nine-month-old report in the *Observer*. Curiously, according to Meltzer, McDevitt never sought a retraction from him. As I like to joke, on its worst day, the *Observer* has dozens of times more readers than my blog has on its best.

---

* My email exchanges with McDevitt, and with both Gary Davis and Jennifer McIntosh of WWE, are included in the companion disk. See "Order the DVD" at the back of this book.

Acknowledgments

Randy Shaw, the publisher of the award-winning San Francisco online alternative newspaper *Beyond Chron*, regularly gave me space for guest columns on topics related to this book. So did Greg Oliver, the producer of the online *SLAM! Wrestling* (and one of my three co-authors of *Benoit: Wrestling with the Horror That Destroyed a Family and Crippled a Sport*). I'm grateful to both Randy and Greg.

Dave Meltzer also ran a couple of guest columns by me on the *Wrestling Observer* website and, more importantly, supported my work in his own way, through various disagreements and misunderstandings.

Karl Olson of Levy, Ram & Olson in San Francisco, one of the country's top First Amendment attorneys, counseled me wisely through World Wrestling Entertainment's legal threats. I know it's only a matter of time before Karl is on the right side on the issue of freelance writers' electronic rights, as well. . . .

Michael Holmes, my editor at ECW Press, was rock-solid, as ever.

When the Stamford Police Department stonewalled

release of the interrogation of the "Benoit Wikipedia hacker," I turned to a network of First Amendment stalwarts. My old friend Joel Simon, executive director of the Committee to Protect Journalists — a New York-based nonprofit promoting press freedom worldwide — introduced me to CPJ staffer Bill Sweeney, a veteran Connecticut reporter who tipped me to the state's exceptionally strong public information law and infrastructure. Peter Scheer of the California First Amendment Coalition helped put me in contact with Stephanie Reitz of the Associated Press, the former "sunshine chair" of the Connecticut chapter of the Society of Professional Journalists, and her successor Steve Kalb of the Connecticut Radio Network. Stephanie and Steve, in turn, referred me to the knowledgeable staff of the Connecticut Freedom of Information Commission. Thanks to all of you.

Two literary betters, Frank Deford and Samuel G. Freedman — my name doesn't belong in the same sentence as theirs — gave me important encouragement and support early on. Author, public radio commentator, and probably the greatest magazine sports writer of all time, Frank belies the adage that nice guys finish last. Sam is the prolific journalist and author who teaches the legendary course on nonfiction book writing at the Columbia University Graduate School of Journalism, in which I have never enrolled. (For one reason, I can't. Psst: Don't tell Sam that I dropped out of college a semester before graduation.)

My cousin Dan Muchnick and his gracious wife Juli helped with the logistics of public records collection in the Atlanta area. Not only that — Dan still picked up the dinner tab when I later had the great opportunity to reconnect with them on my Georgia research trip. Dan and I both wonder what his father and my uncle, St. Louis promoter and National Wrestling Alliance president Sam Muchnick, would have thought of this book.

Friends Scott Townsend, of Santa Rosa, and Connor McDonald, of Berkeley, more than once saved my technologically challenged derriere on computer and audiovisual issues.

Thanks for their general support to Charles Chalmers, Jerry Karabel, Josh Kornbluth, Alice Sunshine, Kim Wood. Thanks for specific support to Dave Gee (book cover design) and Jake Meltzer (my Web 2.0 guru).

Though our roles were sometimes adversarial, I appreciated the professionalism of several public servants in Fayette County. Most importantly, Katye Vogt, the CAD records manager of the Fayette County 911 Communications Center, drilled into her files three different times in response to my queries until I was finally satisfied that I had in hand the audio of all the Benoit-related calls from June 25, 2007. Rick Lindsey, a Peachtree City attorney who represented the Fayette County Sheriff's Office, walked a fine line in his thankless task of administering the release of public records. I realize that listing Vogt and Lindsey here could cause them collateral grief. But as they've already learned, my own medicine chest includes a spoonful of mischief.

Mel Hutnick, an attorney in Belleville, Illinois, and a former prosecutor, spent hours on the phone with me as I rehashed new findings and reflected on scenarios. Mel is a mutual friend of Larry Matysik, wrestling author, promoter, and Sam Muchnick's long-time right-hand man and eventual biographer. I mention Mel not only to memorialize his generosity but also because, in one of our conversations, he uttered the line that best captures the ambiguous essence of an examination of the warps of a bizarre lifestyle and industry, and what they tell us about contemporary American society.

Something very disturbing was going on after that double murder-suicide on Green Meadow Lane. The exact nature of that something? That is for you, the reader, to decide. As Mel Hutnick put it, "Sometimes you just have to leave the participles dangling."

Irvin Muchnick
Berkeley, California
January 2009

About the Author

Irvin Muchnick (www.muchnick.net) is the author of *Wrestling Babylon: Piledriving Tales of Drugs, Sex, Death, and Scandal*, and co-author of *Benoit: Wrestling with the Horror That Destroyed a Family and Crippled a Sport* (both ECW Press, 2007). A native of St. Louis, he now lives in California, where he fights "only when I have to." He is the lead respondent in the landmark 2009 Supreme Court case on freelance writers' rights, *Reed Elsevier v. Muchnick*.

About the Photos

Pages 1–2: all photos courtesy of Bob Leonard.

Page 3: Photos courtesy of Mike Lano.

Page 3: Nancy Benoit with Too Cold Scorpio and Sandman in ECW (ECW Press archives).

Page 4: George Napolitano.

Pages 5–6: all photos courtesy Mike Lano.

Page 7: Eddie Geurerro, courtesy Jake Aurelian.

Page 7: Johnny Grunge and Rocco Rock, courtesy Mike Lano.

Pages 8–9: Simon Dean, courtesy Mike Lano; Randy Orton and Umaga, courtesy Matt Balk; all other photos courtesy Mike Mastrandrea.

Page 10: Vince McMahon (ECW Press archives).

Page 10 Michelle McCool, courtesy Matt Balk.

Page 13: Chavo Guerrero and Kane, courtesy Mike Mastrandrea.

Page 13: Scott Armstrong, courtesy Matt Balk.

Page 13: Dave Taylor Singing with Paul Burchill, courtesy Shawn Boyette.

Page 14: All photos courtesy AP.

Page 15: Linda McMahon, (ECW Press archives).

Page 16: Chris Benoit, 2004, courtesy Jake Aurelian.

Order the DVD

A companion DVD with further documentation of information in this book can be ordered separately. It is not a movie DVD; it is on a DVD disk only because the total volume of the files exceeds the capacity of a standard CD. Below is the list of files. To order the disk, send $20 (U.S. orders), $25 U.S. (Canadian orders), or $30 U.S. (all other foreign orders) to:

BENOIT BOOK DVD
P.O. Box 9629
Berkeley, California 94709

If an email address is included with the order, an email acknowledgment will be sent prior to filling the order. (Orders can also be placed by remitting the appropriate payment, via PayPal, to paypal@muchnick.net.) Shipping is by standard postal service.

LIST OF FILES
• Georgia Bureau of Investigation Medical Examiner's autopsy report

- Complete set of crime scene photos (these do not include the corpses)
- Audio of 911 calls
- Audio of home answering machine messages
- Royal Canadian Mounted Police report containing the earliest official documentation of murder-suicide
- Full text of World Wrestling Entertainment road agent Fit Finlay's report to the office on the June 23, 2007, show in Beaumont, Texas
- Full text of the email exchanges between author Irvin Muchnick and Fayette County Sheriff's Detective Ethon Harper
- Sheriff's report logs of the text messages to and from Chris and Nancy Benoit's cell phones
- The file of author Irvin Muchnick's Connecticut Freedom of Information Commission complaint against the Stamford police
- Summary of Georgia Bureau of Investigation Medical Examiner's toxicology report
- Full text of the email exchanges between author Irvin Muchnick and WWE personnel: vice president for corporation communications Gary Davis, head of publicity Jennifer McIntosh, and attorney Jerry McDevitt